TRANSFORMATION

THE HEART OF PAUL'S GOSPEL

Snapshots

Michael F. Bird, Series Editor

David A. deSilva

LEXHAM PRESS

Transformation: The Heart of Paul's Gospel
Snapshots

Lexham Press, 1313 Commercial St., Bellingham, WA 98225
LexhamPress.com

ISBN 978-1-57-799585-2

Series Editor: Michael F. Bird
Assistant Editors: Claire Brubaker, Lynnea Fraser, Abigail Stocker
Cover Design: Christine Gerhart
Typesetting: ProjectLuz.com

In memory of Dr. James E. Ridgway Sr. (1932–2014),

founder and former president of Educational Opportunities Tours

TABLE OF CONTENTS

Abbreviations..ix

Introduction: Hearing the Whole of Paul's Good News...........................1

Chapter 1..7
FOUNDATIONS FOR A BROADER UNDERSTANDING OF
PAUL'S GOSPEL OF TRANSFORMATION

Transformation in Paul's Proclamation of Good News............10

The Necessity of Transformation:
"There Is No Favoritism with God" (Rom 2:11) 14

The Necessity of Transformation: Paul Places Conditions
on Salvation beyond Mere Belief 19

What Does "Justification" Involve for Paul? 24

Once Saved, Always Saved—but When "Saved"?
Salvation as a "Work in Process"...35

A Great Gift Is a Great Responsibility 38

Chapter 2 44
THE GOSPEL MEANS THE TRANSFORMATION OF THE INDIVIDUAL:
YOU ARE FREE TO BECOME A NEW PERSON IN CHRIST

You Were Freed for a Fresh Start with God 45

You Were Freed from Being Who You Were to
Become Holy and Just in God's Sight 48

You Were Freed to Live a Life of Doing Good 50

Transformation Means a Putting Off and a Putting On 53

God Makes This Transformation Possible through the
Gift of the Holy Spirit 58

You Are Free from the Fear of Death 63

Chapter 3 67

THE GOSPEL MEANS THE TRANSFORMATION OF COMMUNITY:
YOU ARE FREE TO RELATE TO ONE ANOTHER IN NEW WAYS

The Transformation of Strangers into Family,
Many Bodies into One Body 68

Paul's Guidance for Living as a Transformed and
Transforming Community 72

Restorative Intervention...73

Prioritizing Reconciliation 74

Sharing Like Family 76

Investing in and Encouraging One Another 77

Moving from Self-Centered Rights to
Other-Centered Restraint 78

Breaking through Ethnic Barriers, Classes,
Castes, and Gender Lines 80

No Room for Partisanship 84

Christian Families within the Christian Family............87

Conclusion..91

Chapter 4 93

THE GOSPEL MEANS THE TRANSFORMATION OF THE COSMOS:
YOU ARE FREE FROM THE WORLD'S RULES TO WITNESS
TO GOD'S RULE

The "World" as Problem 94

The Transformation of Our Relationship to the *Kosmos*........102

The Transformation of Creation Itself 111

Subject and Author Index...117

Scripture Index 123

ABBREVIATIONS

Scripture Versions

CEB	Common English Bible
ESV	English Standard Version
HCSB	Holman Christian Standard Bible
NIV	New International Version
NRSV	New Revised Standard Version

Apocrypha and Septuagint

Sir	Sirach/Ecclesiasticus
Tob	Tobit
Wis	Wisdom of Solomon

Old Testament Pseudepigrapha

1 En.	1 Enoch
T. Job.	Testament of Job

Greek and Latin Works

Ad M. Caes.	Fronto, Ad Marcum Caesarem
Ap. (Josephus)	Josephus, Against Apion
Ant. (Josephus)	Josephus, Jewish Antiquities
Ben.	Seneca, De beneficiis
Rhod.	Dio Chrysostom, Rhodaica (Or. 31)

Pol.	Aristotle, *Politica*
Contempl.	Philo, *De vita contemplativa*
Decal.	Philo, *De decalogo*

Commentary Series and Journals

BECNT	Baker Evangelical Commentary on the New Testament
JBL	*Journal of Biblical Literature*
JSNT	*Journal for the Study of the New Testament*
NIGTC	New International Greek Testament Commentary
NTS	*New Testament Studies*
WBC	Word Biblical Commentary

Hearing the Whole of Paul's Good News

As Paul traveled throughout the eastern Mediterranean, he was driven by a message he found so compelling that he became essentially a rootless wanderer. He went wherever a door for proclaiming this message opened for him—willingly enduring all hardships, any deprivation, to advance what he was convinced was God's decisive intervention on behalf of humanity.

What was this "good news" that he announced throughout Syria, Turkey, Greece, and eventually even in Rome and possibly in areas further west? "You can be sure that, if you were to die tonight, you would go to heaven"; "If you trust Jesus, all your sins will be forgiven, and you'll be guaranteed a 'not guilty' verdict at the Last Judgment"; "Jesus died in your place, so now you don't need to be afraid of God, of judgment, or of death"; "All you need to do is to confess Jesus as your savior and believe in his name, and you can be sure that you're saved."

There's truth in each of these statements, supported by one or more passages from Paul's writings. It has long concerned me, however, that Christians often fail to connect these statements with passages in Paul's letters that flesh out his larger understanding of how God has provided—out of his sheer goodness and generosity toward us—for our reconciliation, restoration, and rescue from the consequences of having participated in our race's rebellion against God's rule. To understand

Paul's "good news," we need to listen to the *whole* of his message and to make sure in particular that we give due attention to those things he says that don't really fit in with many (especially) Protestant constructs of Paul's theology, lest we privilege our theology above the words of the apostle.

In this book I wish to suggest that Paul's good news could be better summarized in a statement such as the following (as opposed to the statements above): "God offers you the means to become reconciled with him and to become a new person who will want and love and do what is pleasing to him because the Spirit of his Son will live in you and *change* you. The result of God's kindness and activity is that you will live a new kind of life now and, after death, live forever with him."

As I have come to understand Paul's message, it is all about *change*. The good news is nothing less than that God has set in motion the forces and factors that can transform all of creation and make it new, good, and right once again—including *us*. This transformation remains from beginning to end a work of God's favor or "grace," for it begins at God's initiative; it transpires through the working and the power of the gift that God has given, namely the Spirit; and it is brought to completion because of God's commitment and faithfulness. But the accent remains on *transformation* as God's goal for God's gifts and as the result in our lives and churches if we have not "received God's grace for nothing," to borrow a phrase from 2 Cor 6:1, or if we do not "set aside God's grace," to borrow a phrase from Gal 2:21.

What does it mean, for Paul, to receive "the abundance of [God's] grace and of the gift of righteousness" (Rom 5:17)? I want to make a case for this possibility: The "gift of righteousness" is God's gift of the means and power to be changed from the inside out and from the outside in by the working of the Holy Spirit that God gave us and that Jesus died to procure for us (Gal 3:14). It is the gift of being transformed into people who think, speak, and do what is right and pleasing and approved in God's estimation. *This* is the "gift of God" that brings "eternal life" to those who trust (Rom 6:23). If this was indeed a major facet of the gospel that Paul proclaimed, then those who focus on Paul's gospel as essentially pertaining to the free gift of forgiveness of sins and forensic justification may be setting their expectations for what God desires and is able to do within believers and in the midst of the believing community far too low.

I do not presume to have Paul all figured out. Paul's theology is quite complex, made frightfully more complex by two millennia of people commenting on Paul and offering their own reconstructions of his theology. But I am dissatisfied with some of the constructions of Paul's gospel out there, particularly insofar as I do not see these constructions giving due weight to many of the passages that I will bring to the fore in the following chapters. My own construction may well also be deemed inadequate, but I will be satisfied if the reader leaves this book only with a commitment to think afresh about how these other texts inform the gospel's promises and its claims on the believer.

There is a model for the essence of Paul's gospel that commands attention simply on the basis of its pervasive influence in the global Church—the model often referred to as the "Romans Road," which outlines, in logical progression, a proposed path to salvation. This model was a formative influence on my own theology as a young Christian, when it was communicated in the form of printed tracts. Now it is communicated, I would suppose far more widely, by means of the Internet. A query on "Romans Road" results in 27 million hits on Google, bearing witness to a massive Internet presence for this way of talking about the essence of Paul's gospel. There's some variation, but the basic outline is as follows:

1. All have sinned and fall short of God's glory (Rom 3:23).

2. The punishment for sin is eternal death, but the free gift of God is eternal life through Jesus (Rom 6:23).

3. God demonstrated his love for us by sending his Son to die on our behalf even while we were still sinners and enemies (Rom 5:9).

4. The person who believes in his or her heart and confesses with his or her lips that Jesus Christ is Lord will be saved (Rom 10:9).

5. Such people will not face condemnation for their sins (Rom 8:1) and will enjoy peace with God (Rom 5:1).

Each of these paving stones in the Romans Road is solid enough. I would object only to the absence of a good many other such stones that Paul himself laid out when he first paved not the Romans Road but Romans (as well as his other letters). It is to the task of excavating and restoring these stones to their proper place in Paul's understanding of the gospel that this book is committed.

There is another dynamic at work in popular assessments of Paul's gospel that bears mention, since this dynamic is further at variance with Paul's own words. It is not so much the steps in the Romans Road that run afoul of Paul's own proclamation as the excessive and careless claims that some Christians make on the basis of one or more of these steps. The author of the text on one website claims, "Because of Jesus' death on our behalf, we will never be condemned for our sins."[1] This same author draws the further conclusion that, "because of Jesus' death on our behalf, all we have to do is believe in Him, trusting His death as the payment for our sins—and we will be saved!"[2] Another author rejects the claim that "a person must depart from their sinful lifestyle and commit their life to live for God," because "all God requires of us to receive the free gift of eternal life is that we come by way of His only begotten Son, Jesus Christ."[3]

Such statements can only be made at the cost of failing to hear—and failing to heed—statements that Paul himself makes concerning the human response to the grace of God in Jesus Christ. Jesus' death on our behalf does not mean that "all we have to do is believe in Him." Rather Jesus "died for all in order that those who continued living might no longer continue living for themselves, but for him who died and was raised for them" (2 Cor 5:15). Committing oneself to Jesus in trust also means leaving behind sin and living for God: "Stop offering any parts of yourself to Sin as tools of wrongdoing, but offer yourselves to God as people living from among the dead and offer every part of who you are to God as tools of righteousness" (Rom 6:13). Paul grounds the promise

1. "What Is the Romans Road to Salvation?" GotQuestions.org, accessed February 24, 2014, www.gotquestions.org/Romans-road-salvation.html.

2. Ibid.

3. David J. Stewart, "The Romans Road," accessed February 24, 2014, www.jesus-is-savior.com/Basics/romans_road.htm.

that those who are in Christ Jesus will not come into condemnation not just in Jesus' death for our sins but also in the Holy Spirit's activity in leading those in Christ to live in a manner that fulfills God's just decrees: "There is now no condemnation for those who are in Christ Jesus" *because* God has made it possible "that the just requirement of the law might be fulfilled in us, who persevere in walking in line with the Spirit rather than in line with the flesh" (Rom 8:1, 4).

A major problem in Pauline theology today—major not primarily because it is advanced among theologians or scholars but because it has taken deep roots and is confidently promoted throughout the Christian Church—is the tendency to reduce Paul's gospel to something far more limited, far less pervasive, far less *invasive* in terms of what God seeks to do within and through those who put their faith in Jesus than Paul's own written testimony suggests. The result is that what *having faith* in Jesus even means is not itself well understood, since faith, to *be* faith at all, entails a wholehearted commitment to the person of Christ that must also transform the life of a person. Paul's understanding of the call to discipleship (the call to a living, saving faith) did not differ from Jesus' own call—which was not "believe in the effectiveness of my death and resurrection, and you'll be saved no matter what" but "If any want to become my followers, let them deny themselves and take up their cross and follow me. For those who want to save their life will lose it, and those who lose their life for my sake, and for the sake of the gospel, will save it" (Mark 8:34–35).

The goal of this short book, then, is to propose a way of thinking about Paul's gospel—Paul's vision for what God is seeking to bring about through the death and resurrection of his Son, the indwelling of his Spirit, and his future intervention in cosmic affairs—that preserves more fully and more explicitly Paul's own emphases on the transformation of the individual, the community of faith, and the cosmos itself as God's goal for God's saving action, indeed, as "salvation" itself. This presentation remains conversant with Pauline scholarship, most explicitly throughout the opening chapter but also implicitly throughout the sections that follow, which are based on long reflection on Paul's

Letters and interaction with scholarship thereon.[4] In this book, I seek, however, not merely to present the state of the conversation but to engage constructively within that conversation to present a different core metaphor for holding together the various elements of Paul's message and theology.

The first chapter will propose "transformation" as an appropriate overarching framework for thinking about Paul's gospel on the basis of the pervasiveness of this theme, and even this language, throughout Paul's written work. I will follow this up with an exploration of five other facets of Paul's proclamation that, though they tend to recede or even disappear in some constructions of Paul's message, can be more fully and openly incorporated into a construction of Paul's gospel that is centered on transformation. Successive chapters will lay out Paul's vision for the transformation of the individual, of the community of faith, and of the cosmos as the essence of the "good news" that he has perceived and that he proclaimed throughout the Mediterranean as apostle to the nations. The guiding principle for this investigation is that no theology is so sacred as to sit above ongoing examination on the basis of what Paul actually wrote. It thus hopes to continue the tradition of *semper reformanda* at the heart of the Reformation and thus Protestant theology itself.

---

4. See my previous work in this area in *An Introduction to the New Testament: Contexts, Methods & Ministry Formation* (Downers Grove, IL: InterVarsity Press, 2004), 475–775; and *Global Readings: A Sri Lankan Commentary on Paul's Letter to the Galatians* (Eugene, OR: Wipf & Stock, 2011).

CHAPTER 1

Foundations for a Broader Understanding of Paul's Gospel of Transformation

An important development in reflection on Paul's theology was the formulation of "justification" and "sanctification" as two distinct categories for understanding Paul's thought. In many systematic theologies, "justification" refers to the process of being made right with God, often specifically in the sense of receiving a verdict of "not guilty" (that is, being accounted as "righteous") at the judgment, a verdict that is anticipated now on the basis of trusting in Jesus. "Sanctification" refers to the process by which we become holy (or begin to live out the holiness also imputed to us in our conversion). These can be helpful heuristic categories, and they also have the benefit of reflecting language that Paul himself uses in his own exposition of the gospel. These categories, however, can take on a life of their own, constraining our understanding of Paul's writings rather than facilitating our encounter with Paul's own conceptualization of the gospel. In the tradition of the Reformation, however, Scripture must always weigh more heavily than theological tradition. If the latter becomes the controlling force in interpreting the former, we have moved back into the dynamic from which the classic Reformers sought to free the Western church.

One of the less helpful results of the formulation of "justification" and "sanctification" as distinct categories is a tendency to regard the former as the more important when thinking about "salvation" and the latter as more important for thinking about "Christian living." This is not always the case in theological traditions springing from the Reformation. The Anglican bishop J. C. Ryle, for example, makes the bold claim:

> Both [justification and sanctification] are alike necessary to salvation. No one ever reached heaven without a renewed heart as well as forgiveness, without the Spirit's grace as well as the blood of Christ, without a meetness for eternal glory as well as a title. The one is just as necessary as the other.[1]

When Paul himself speaks about "what counted" in God's sight, he speaks about "being a new creation," which Klyne Snodgrass says "for Paul meant a life of faith working through love [Gal 5:6], and outside the context of the debate over 'works righteousness,' this could even be described as a life of keeping the commandments of God [1 Cor 7:19]."[2] In the eyes of Ryle and Snodgrass, what normally falls under the heading of "sanctification" remains very much in the center of the salvation that God seeks to bring about.

Some traditions are less insistent about the essential nature of sanctification, though they still affirm its importance as a demonstration of the quality of the faith that the believer possesses, i.e., as an indication that his or her "faith" is *indeed* "faith." In the Thirty-Nine Articles of Religion that form the historic confession of the Church of England, for example, "justification" and "good works" are treated as separate articles, with the latter contributing to the former only the demonstration of the quality of one's faith as "true and lively." The twelfth article

---

1. J. C. Ryle, *Holiness: Its Nature, Difficulties, Hindrances, and Roots* (London: William Hunt, 1883), 30.
2. Klyne R. Snodgrass, "Justification by Grace—to the Doers: An Analysis of the Place of Romans 2 in the Theology of Paul," *NTS* 32 (1986): 72-93, 86. Also relevant is the observation of Simon Gathercole ("A Law unto Themselves: The Gentiles in Romans 2.14-15 Revisited," [*JSNT* 24 (2002): 27-49], 48): "In the company of statements about the reward of eternal life for obedience in 2.7, 10, 26-27, and 29, Rom. 2.13-16 must point to a stronger theology of final vindication on the basis of an obedient life than is evident in most analyses of Pauline theology."

("On Good Works") stresses the importance of such demonstration but not its necessity. The practical result is that "justification" can be too easily conceptualized apart from the idea of the transformation of the person.[3] This is by no means the *necessary* result, but it is all too often the actual result, to which (as we saw in the introduction to this book) many "Romans Road" websites bear witness in their focus on justification (and that in a very limited sense!). At best this leaves sanctification entirely to follow-up and at worst neglects it completely.

I am increasingly of the opinion that Paul himself would have been troubled by the creation of these two categories as discrete stages in an "order of salvation" in the first place, especially where what falls under the heading of "justification" is privileged as the one *necessary* step in this progression. I suspect that a tendency like that of Martin Luther to speak of a more integrated whole would have been preferable for the apostle. According to Mark Seifrid, "because [Luther] regards justification as effecting the new creation, he is able to encompass the whole of the Christian life within its scope.... In contrast to later Protestant thought, in which salvation was divided up into an *ordo salutis*, it remains for Luther a single divine act."[4] The existence of justification and sanctification as distinct categories threatens to rend asunder what Paul joins together in his vision of a single, great process of God's intervention in the lives of human beings.

3. These same articles survive among the Twenty-Five Articles of Religion of the Methodist Church, into which John Wesley did *not* interject his doctrine of perfection, which came close to recapturing the dynamic of Paul's theology of transformation. Reformed theologian and biblical scholar Michael Bird articulates a similar position, though more forcefully in regard to the importance of a life of doing what is pleasing to God as an essential sign of genuine faith in Christ: "The works that are performed in-Christ as empowered by the Spirit demonstrate the integrity of the faith that the believer professes. Any good by us stems from Christ's work in us. ... Works as christologically conceived, pneumatically empowered, and divinely endowed are necessary for salvation in so far as they reveal the character of authentic faith expressed in the form of obedience, love, faithfulness, righteousness and holiness" (*The Saving Righteousness of God: Studies on Paul, Justification and the New Perspective* [Milton Keynes, UK: Paternoster, 2007], 178).
4. Mark Seifrid, "Paul's Use of Righteousness Language against Its Hellenistic Background," in *Justification and Variegated Nomism*, ed. D. A. Carson, P. T. O'Brien, and Mark Seifrid, vol. 2, *The Paradoxes of Paul* (Mohr Siebeck: Tübingen, and Grand Rapids: Baker Academic, 2001), 71. Adolf Schlatter also complained about "parceling out God's grace" into so many discrete categories as if the divine action could be broken down into the divine "to-do list" of an *ordo salutis* (*Das Christliche Dogma* [Stuttgart: Calwer, 1923], 601n279).

Several observations, each based on multiple and often extensive passages from the writings of Paul, lead me in this direction. First, Paul speaks of our transformation as the goal of his preaching and of God's intervention, not merely about our acquittal (whether initial, final, or both). Second, such transformation is essential, because God will not show favoritism in the judgment. Third, Paul clearly attaches conditions to our attaining God's goal for us beyond settling upon a certain belief and making a certain confession, which has bearing on what "faith" means for Paul in such formulations as "justified by faith." Fourth, Paul talks about "justification" as the result of having been brought in line with God's righteousness and as a future experience of being acquitted at the Last Judgment on the basis of a life lived *as well as* an accomplished event of being reconciled to God after our estrangement in sin. Any assessment of Paul's gospel must account for the connection between initial and final justification. Fifth, Paul also speaks of "salvation" as something we will enjoy or experience in the future, not merely as something already accomplished. Again, any assessment of Paul's gospel has to take this whole range of usage into account. Sixth and finally, God expects us not just to "receive" his gifts but to make the use of and response to his gifts that show an appropriate assessment of their value—in this case, a life for a life! If these are indeed correct observations, as the following sections will seek to establish, then Paul understood God to be seeking to accomplish far more than many Christians realize and, as a possible consequence, allow to take place in their own lives.

TRANSFORMATION IN PAUL'S PROCLAMATION OF GOOD NEWS

As Paul reflects on God's saving intervention in his own life, on the results of his having trusted in Jesus, and on his quest to be justified before God through the way opened up by Jesus, he writes:

> I died to the Torah through the Torah in order that I might live to God. I was crucified together with Christ; it's no longer *me* living, but *Christ* living in me. The life I'm living

now in the flesh, I live in faith toward the Son of God who
loved me and gave himself up for me. (Gal 2:19-20)

Paul speaks of a dramatic and real change in his life. As he looks upon
his life, he sees that the person he was is no longer driving or shaping
his being or his practice. Instead Jesus Christ himself has taken on flesh
in a new way in Paul, making Paul into a new person—a Christ-directed
person, an extension of Christ's own willing, being, and doing. This, I
would propose, is Paul's description of the justified life. Indeed, the verses preceding these, namely Gal 2:15-18, provide one of Paul's densest
discussions of justification through trusting Jesus as opposed to shaping one's life after Torah-prescribed practices.[5] This description of the
justified life is a description of a *transformed* life. The person brought in
line with God's righteousness is the person whose flesh Christ himself
has taken on.

In a second passage where Paul speaks very personally about his
desire for the righteousness found through attachment to Jesus as
opposed to the Torah, he uses language even more closely reflective
of transformation:

> On account of Christ I have written off everything as a
> loss and consider it all to be sewage in order that I may
> win Christ and be found in him, not having my own righ-
> teousness attained on the basis of the Torah but attained
> through trusting Jesus—God's righteousness attained on
> the basis of trust—in order to know him and the power of
> his resurrection and the fellowship of his sufferings, be-
> ing reshaped in connection with him (*symmorphizomenos*)
> into the likeness of his death, if somehow I might arrive at
> the resurrection from the dead. (Phil 3:8-11)

---

5. Several commentaries offer helpful guidance on the interpretation of these verses. See, e.g.,
F. F. Bruce, *Galatians*, NIGTC (Grand Rapids: Eerdmans, 1982), 135-47; Richard Longenecker,
Galatians, WBC (Dallas: Word, 1990), 80-96; James D. G. Dunn, *The Epistle to the Galatians*
(London: A. C. Black, 1993), 131-50; Ben Witherington III, *Grace in Galatia: A Commentary on
Paul's Letter to the Galatians* (Grand Rapids: Eerdmans, 1998), 169-96; David A. deSilva, *Global
Readings: A Sri Lankan Commentary on Paul's Letter to the Galatians* (Eugene, OR: Wipf & Stock,
2011), 112-36.

Two points are of special importance in this passage. First, becoming like Jesus, and especially being *morphed* into the self-giving obedience Jesus displayed in his own obedience unto death (see Phil 2:5–11), is a process integral and essential to knowing Jesus (that is, having any kind of relationship with him) and to being found righteous "in him." Second, it is a process integral and essential to sharing in his resurrection (hence, entering into eternal life). This is fully in keeping with other statements by Paul suggesting that dying with Christ is a prerequisite to rising with Christ, language that Paul always uses with ethical implications—that is, that such dying means the transformation of our lives and practice (most notably in Rom 6:1–23).

Paul applies this language of transformation to his converts either as his own goal for them or as God's overarching purpose for them in no fewer than four of his letters. In Galatians he is particularly exercised as he finds his converts succumbing to the arguments of rival teachers that perhaps Gentile believers really do need to become Jews through circumcision and other Torah-prescribed practices if they want to line up with God's righteousness.[6] At one point he exclaims, "My little children, with whom I am in labor again until Christ is formed (*morphōthē*) within you!" (Gal 4:19). This image, expressed when Paul is at a raw and emotional point because of what he believes to be at stake, suggests again that the most essential thing for Paul is that Christ take shape within his disciples, just as Christ had taken shape and taken on fresh life in Paul (Gal 2:19–20). In this moment, Paul reveals that his mission is not essentially about "winning souls" or "getting people off the hook at the Last Judgment." It is primarily about working with people to surrender themselves to this work of God, this deep and fundamental transformation whereby their lives cease to be what they *were* and begin to be an extension of *Christ's own* willing, being, and doing.

---

6. On the pastoral situation in Galatia and the "gospel" of Paul's rivals, see Bruce, *Galatians*, 19–32; Longenecker, *Galatians*, lxxxviii–c; Dunn, *Galatians*, 9–19; Witherington, *Grace in Galatia*, 21–25; deSilva, *Global Readings*, 8–20.

A similar image of God's work in the new covenant emerges in Paul's second surviving letter to the churches in Corinth.[7] At the climax of an argument concerning the superiority of the new covenant to the covenant mediated through Moses—an argument that interestingly never uses the terminology of justification or works or even faith—Paul declares that "we all, gazing at the Lord's glory with unveiled face [i.e., seeing his glory without a veil over his face], are being transformed (*metamorphoumetha*) into the same image from glory to glory as [something coming about] from the Lord, the Spirit" (2 Cor 3:18). The Greek word translated as "we are being transformed" survives as a loan word in English as "metamorphosis," and this very much captures Paul's vision for what God seeks to bring about through the new covenant. When we trust Jesus as our deliverer and look to his death and resurrection as the means of our own forgiveness and welcome into a good eternity, our mortal selves must become the cocoon within which a great metamorphosis transpires. The analogy is imperfect, of course, since there is no actual cocoon within which to retreat and hide the process from third parties. The process of transformation will be entirely visible, which is often a point of embarrassment for Christians since the process is slow and not consistently forward-moving, but the changes that *are* effected in us are also a vivid testimony to the power and righteousness of God at work.

In a number of his writings Paul uses a related image for this transformation that is at the core of God's work within and among us—the image of the believer stripping off one set of clothing and wrapping another set around him- or herself. The clothing represents quite explicitly the person we once were and the person we are becoming in Christ.

> You were taught to put away your former way of life, your old self, corrupt and deluded by its lusts, and to be renewed in the spirit of your minds [see also Rom 12:1-2], and to clothe yourselves with the new self, created according to

---

7. Paul wrote at least four letters to the churches in Corinth. In 1 Cor 5:9 he refers to a previous letter of his that had occasioned some misunderstanding; in 2 Corinthians (2:1-4, 9; 7:8) he refers to a painful letter that he had sent after he had sent 1 Corinthians and after he had made a subsequent visit to the congregation.

the likeness of God in true righteousness and holiness. (Eph 4:22–24 NRSV)[8]

This is an eloquent exposition of what it means to be a new creation. Becoming "a new creation" is what Paul celebrates as coming into being when a person is "in Christ" (2 Cor 5:17) and what Paul claims *alone* has value in God's sight, as opposed to whether a person is circumcised or otherwise conforms to the distinctive practices prescribed by the law of Moses (Gal 6:15).

Finally, Paul speaks of this transformation as central to God's purposes for those who would believe, whose response of trust God foresaw: "Those whom God foreknew he destined to be conformed (*symmorphous*) to the image of his Son, in order that he might be the firstborn among many brothers and sisters" (Rom 8:29). This verse, incidentally, immediately follows the oft-quoted "we know that he works all things together for the good for those who love God, who are called in accordance with God's purpose" (Rom 8:28). Reading these two verses together strongly suggests that "the good" Paul has in mind is specifically this transformation, this meshing, into the image of Jesus (rather than some general "good" such as enables our vague application of the verse to innumerable situations). *This* is what accords with God's overarching purposes for us. This transformation is the "good work" that God has begun in believers and that God "will bring … to completion by the day of Christ Jesus" (Phil 1:6).

The Necessity of Transformation: "There Is No Favoritism with God" (Rom 2:11)

Such transformation of our lives, our practices, our very selves is central to God's purposes for us, indeed to God's purposes in sending his Son to die on our behalf and to be raised again to life—so that God's righteous image, perfectly carried in that Son, might come to life in us through

8. The authenticity of the authorship of Ephesians is a matter of considerable debate in biblical scholarship. For my own assessment of the arguments on either side of this complex issue, see David A. deSilva, *An Introduction to the New Testament: Contexts, Methods & Ministry Formation* (Downers Grove, IL: InterVarsity Press, 2004), 716–21.

the indwelling Spirit of God's Son. It may also very well be central to our final justification in the sense of our acquittal as "righteous" people before the judgment seat of the just God. Here the distinction between "justification" as what happens when we trust in Jesus and "justification" as acquittal on the last day becomes very important to observe. At no point does this work of transformation become "our righteousness" as something we achieve on our own or establish for ourselves (thus Paul's affirmations in Phil 3:9; Rom 10:2–4 continue to have force). The transformation of which Paul speaks is Spirit-empowered and Spirit-directed. It all depends on God's gracious gift of the Holy Spirit, lavished upon us because of Jesus' death on our behalf (Gal 3:3; 5:16–25). There is, nevertheless, a significant gap between thinking that God will acquit us because of the righteousness his Son displayed in first-century Judaea and thinking that God will acquit us because he sees his righteous Son living in, through, and among us when we stand before his judgment seat.

Paul's Letter to the Romans is considered by many to be his manifesto of justification by faith, so it seems appropriate to engage this text in greater depth. Paul is:

> not ashamed of the gospel; it is the power of God for salvation to everyone who has faith, to the Jew first and also to the Greek. For in it the righteousness of God is revealed through faith for faith; as it is written, "The one who is righteous will live by faith." (Rom 1:16–17, citing Hab 2:4)

The connection between this, the "thesis statement" for Romans, and the following verse is often overlooked: "For the wrath of God is revealed from heaven against all ungodliness and wickedness of those who by their wickedness suppress the truth" (Rom 1:16–18 NRSV).

The starting point for Paul's announcement about the manifestation of God's justice or righteousness is an announcement about the manifestation of God's wrath. God's judgment itself is—stunningly—part of Paul's "good news": Paul speaks of "the day when, through Jesus Christ, God will judge the secrets of human beings, *according to the good news I proclaim*" (Rom 2:16). God's burning fury against unjust and evil practices is central to God's character as "just" from the beginning to the end of the scriptural witness. God's triumph over every form of injustice and unrighteousness is "good news" for the cosmos that God created. Paul begins by listing the ways in which Gentiles as a whole were known to act unjustly toward their creator God and to behave in ways that flouted God's holy standards. Owing God the very gift of life itself, already a manifestation of supreme grace on God's part, all human beings were under obligation to use that gift in a manner that brought honor to their divine benefactor and reflected loyalty toward God and an active desire to serve God. Instead, they met God's grace toward them with insult and affront, failing to honor God, giving the honor due God to the no-gods of idols instead and living in such a manner as to flout God's just requirements.

But then he turns to those among his own people who prided themselves on their assurance of God's acceptance without any corresponding claims on their obedience and who looked down on the Gentiles as "outsiders" to God's care and deliverance:

> You say, "We know that God's judgment on those who do such things is in accordance with truth." Do you imagine, whoever you are, that when you judge those who do such things and yet do them yourself, you will escape the judgment of God? Or do you despise the riches of his kindness and forbearance and patience? Do you not realize that God's kindness is meant to lead you to repentance? But by your hard and impenitent heart you are storing up wrath for yourself on the day of wrath, when God's righteous judgment will be revealed. For he will repay according to each one's deeds: to those who by patiently doing good seek for glory and honor and immortality, he will give eternal life; while for those who are self-seeking and who obey not the truth but wickedness, there will be wrath and fury. There will be anguish and distress for everyone who does evil, the Jew first and also the Greek, but glory and honor and peace for everyone who does good, the Jew first and also the Greek. *For God shows no partiality.* (Rom 2:2–11 NRSV, emphasis mine)

Paul is calling into question the idea that God's election of and covenant with the Jewish people exempt them from God's judgment. On the contrary, if God is indeed just and competent to judge the cosmos in righteousness, if there is anything God *cannot* do it would be to show partiality in judgment. Being part of God's holy people is not a free pass through the judgment but an invitation into a covenant community that has clear knowledge of God and what God desires to see in the hearts and practices of those he created. Those who belong to such a community are thus able to reliably learn what God requires and enjoy the social support of a group of like-minded and similarly-informed others in the quest to embody those norms so as to become pleasing to God and to receive God's favorable verdict on their lives. That is an immense privilege, an immense enjoyment of *favor*, but it does not include *favoritism*.

Paul makes a bold claim in Rom 2:2–11. He asserts that what matters to God is our obedience, not the compartment into which we place ourselves or are placed by others, because God does not play favorites. It is not whether one has been circumcised and inducted into the Jewish people that matters (see, again, 1 Cor 7:19; Gal 5:6; 6:15); it is whether one has lived in line with God's righteous standards.

This raises the question of why it should be different in the case of Christians.[9] If God will not show favoritism toward Israel, his historic "chosen people," in the judgment, will God show favoritism toward his Son's friends just because they are his friends? I am reminded of a disturbing letter from the Roman period addressed to Marcus Aurelius when he was just the son of the emperor, before he had become emperor himself. Fronto, a senator and friend of Marcus, asked Marcus to help someone get a favorable verdict before the court of Marcus's father, the emperor.[10] We don't know how Marcus Aurelius replied. It would not have been at all unusual for him to agree, since securing a

---

9. See the provocative essay by Hendrickus Boers, "We Who Are by Inheritance Jews; Not from the Gentiles, Sinners," *JBL* 111 (1992): 273–81, in which he objects to the fact that "through the seal of baptism, Christianity claims for itself the privilege of an exclusive relationship with God, the very privilege which Paul denied the Jews in Romans, as he had done previously in Galatians" (277).

10. Fronto, *Ad M. Caes.* 3.2. See similarly a letter written by Cicero in the late republican period (*Ad Familiares* 13).

verdict through one's connections was just another kind of "favor" a well-placed individual could gain for his or her friends and clients at that time. But though this was a *known* practice, even pagan Greek and Latin ethicists recognized that this was not a *just* practice, and neither was the judge who was so influenced acting "justly." Can Christians really think that God, then, will forget who he is—his character as a "just" judge—just because we call ourselves friends of his Son without doing what he says?

Paul writes further, "Circumcision brings benefit if you put the Torah into practice, but if you are a transgressor of Torah your circumcision has become uncircumcision" (Rom 2:25). Would Paul speak similar works to those who claim Christ and boast in being saved by their reception of the gospel and their baptism, but don't live in line with the commands of the Lord they profess? Would he say "your baptism has become unbaptism"? We know what the Matthean tradition remembers as the answer that Jesus would have given:

> Not everyone who says to me, "Lord, Lord," will enter the kingdom of heaven, but only the one who does the will of my Father in heaven. On that day many will say to me, "Lord, Lord, did we not prophesy in your name, and cast out demons in your name, and do many deeds of power in your name?" Then I will declare to them, "I never knew you; go away from me, you evildoers." (Matt 7:21-23 NRSV)

The disobedience of God's historic people Israel was a blot on God's reputation in the world: "You who boast in the Torah, do you dishonor God by transgressing the Torah? 'For God's name is spoken ill of among the Gentiles because of you,' just as it is written" (Rom 2:23-24, citing Isa 52:5). The same is true when people who claim to belong to Jesus live like people who do not—something that has been noticed by the millennial generation and has turned them off from the church like no other factor.[11]

---

11. See the fascinating but indicting book by David Kinnaman and Gabe Lyons, *unChristian: What a New Generation Really Thinks about Christianity...and Why It Matters* (Grand Rapids: Baker, 2012).

"God does not show favoritism" (Rom 2:11). The authors of the Old and New Testaments—and the books in between—affirm this as a core characteristic of the just Judge (see, e.g., 2 Chr 19:7; Sir 35:13–16; 1 En. 63:8; T. Job 4:7; 43:13; Acts 10:34; Gal 2:6; Eph 6:9; Col 3:25). Paul similarly affirms it concerning God as an absolute, not just as a characteristic about God that is at play for those who don't know his Son. What the gospel, therefore, *cannot* mean is this: When God comes to judge the world, God will treat you as righteous when you are not;[12] you're saved from being judged on that day no matter what you do, how you live, for *whom* you live; Jesus' righteousness is enough to get you off the hook with God; God expects nothing from you. If we think this is what Paul's gospel means for us, we have to be prepared to say that God *does* show partiality. God will judge his Son's friends according to one set of standards and everyone else by another set of standards—and he will declare innocent those in the first group who would fail the test if they belonged to the second group. Such a view is naïve and even unjust on our part. If Paul went to such lengths to negate any claim to privilege before God on the part of the Jewish people, who had a significant pile of scriptural texts to legitimate their claim to enjoy special favor from God, he would not allow us the comfort of believing that God will have a double standard when it comes to Christians at the judgment.

The Necessity of Transformation: Paul Places Conditions on Salvation beyond Mere Belief

It would be rash to make such claims as found in the previous section on the basis of a reading of one paragraph in Romans. A strong thread runs throughout Paul's letters, however, affirming Rom 2:6–11 as a valid statement about Paul's beliefs about God's justice and judgment with regard to Christians along with everybody else. I have heard theologians explain away Rom 2:6–11 by claiming that it is merely a hypothetical

---

12. This is not to deny that, in initial justification, God *does* treat us as righteous when we are not, setting aside our sins against and affronts to God as an act of grace and kindness on the basis of Jesus' self-giving death (see also Rom 4:5–8). But this is the beginning of the long work of God's grace in our lives, not the be-all and end-all of the same. This point is what all the material that follows will seek to demonstrate to be *Paul's* message.

argument about how God judges *prior to* or *apart from* Christ's coming and a person's belief in Jesus. Paul provides testimony throughout his letters suggesting that such theologians are engaging in mere wishful thinking.[13]

Take, for example, the following verses, also from Romans: "For if you keep living in line with the flesh, you are going to die; but if by the Spirit you put to death the deeds of the body, you will live" (Rom 8:13-14). In the final clause Paul is talking quite specifically about living beyond death, sharing in Christ's resurrection, as he says just a few verses ahead of these: "If the Spirit of the one who raised Jesus from the dead lives in you, the one who raised Christ from the dead will also give life to your death-bound bodies through the Spirit that is living in you" (Rom 8:11). The "ifs" are indeed present also in the Greek text and not the result of my taking liberties in translation. Paul is setting *conditions* on entering into the "life" of the resurrection: it is necessary to allow God's Spirit to become the driving force in one's life and to cease to live for oneself. Continuing to feed the passions and drives of self-centered, self-directed living (what Paul speaks of as "the flesh") shipwrecks God's work of transformation and deliverance. On the other hand, yielding ourselves to the transformation God desires to work within us through God's precious gift of the Holy Spirit allows God to complete the work of deliverance that he began in us in our coming to faith. One must be "*led* by the Spirit" to be in fact a "child of God" (Rom 8:14).[14]

In several other letters, Paul lists what he presents as "deal breakers" in terms of deliverance, conceived of here as entrance into God's kingdom:

> The works of the flesh are clearly evident: sexual immorality, uncleanness, shameless debauchery, idolatry, drug-induced spells, enmities, strife, emulation, wrathful

---

13. Michael Bird (*The Saving Righteousness of God: Studies on Paul, Justification and the New Perspective* [Milton Keynes, UK: Paternoster, 2007], 160) also rejects a reading of Rom 2:1-16 that regards the passage as hypothetical only, since "similar statements about works are identifiable elsewhere in Paul's letters (cf. 1 Cor. 2.10-15; 2 Cor. 5.10; Rom 14.10) which are quite evidently not making hypothetical claims."

14. The syntax of the Greek is clear on this point: the verse cannot be inverted to mean "all who are children of God are led by the Spirit."

outbursts, rivalries, divisions, factions, envying, drunken bouts, gluttonous parties, and other things like these. Concerning these things I tell you in advance, just as I warned you before: Those who keep practicing such things will not inherit the kingdom of God. (Gal 5:19–21)

Do you not know that wrongdoers will not inherit the kingdom of God? Do not be deceived! Fornicators, idolaters, adulterers, male prostitutes, sodomites, thieves, the greedy, drunkards, revilers, robbers—none of these will inherit the kingdom of God. And this is what some of you used to be. But you were washed, you were sanctified, you were justified in the name of the Lord Jesus Christ and in the Spirit of our God. (1 Cor 6:9–11 NRSV)

Be sure of this, that no fornicator or impure person, or one who is greedy (that is, an idolater), has any inheritance in the kingdom of Christ and of God. Let no one deceive you with empty words, for because of these things the wrath of God comes on those who are disobedient. (Eph 5:5 6 NRSV)

What would these "empty words" be? The context in Ephesians suggests rather clearly that they have to do with denying the consequences of continuing to live for oneself, one's own interests, one's own gratification (thus, continuing to make room for fornication, impurity, and greed, Eph 5:5). These "empty words" would include affirmations that God doesn't require a complete reorientation of one's life; that God is content to let people "slide by" on a public confession, an interior "belief" or claim about Jesus' death on our behalf, and some splashing of water; that our behavior doesn't really matter for salvation because that would make it somehow dependent on works. On the contrary, we need to begin to reckon seriously with the fact that "judgment by works is *integral to* Paul's theology and not merely an inconsistent anomaly."[15]

It is important to make a distinction at this point between failures in the course of discipleship and failing to pursue transformation. In the passage from Gal 5:19-21, Paul makes it clear that he is not talking about those who fall perchance into any of these sins, as we all in fact do; he is talking about those who *continue* in these practices, who make ongoing room to engage in them rather than recognizing them as contrary to God's righteousness and desires for us, and seeking the Spirit's guidance and empowerment to leave those attitudes and practices behind. Paul makes this even clearer just a few verses later in the same letter:

> Don't deceive yourselves: God is not mocked. For whatever a person sows, that shall he or she also reap: because the one who *keeps on sowing* to his or her flesh will harvest decay from the flesh, but the one who *keeps on sowing* to the Spirit will harvest eternal life from the Spirit. Let us not grow tired of doing what is noble, for we will reap the harvest in its proper season if we don't give up. As long as we have a season, then, let us work what is good toward all, and especially toward those who belong to the household of faith. (Gal 6:7-10)

Transformation is an *essential* process, but it is still a *process* (one that is opposed to the process of living for oneself). From Paul's point of view, moreover, there are really only two directions for our investment of ourselves — feeding the agenda of the "flesh" and feeding the agenda of the "Spirit." He urges his readers to bring integrity to their lives rather than allowing themselves to be pulled in two contrary directions. He

---

15. Bird, *Saving Righteousness*, 159, versus E. P. Sanders, *Paul, the Law, and the Jewish People* (Philadelphia: Fortress, 1983), 123-36; H. Räisänen, *Paul and the Law*, 2nd ed. (Tübingen: Mohr Siebeck, 1993), 101-07. N. T. Wright (*Justification: God's Plan and Paul's Vision* [Downers Grove, IL: InterVarsity Press, 2009], 184-85) also cites several of these passages alongside yet others to demonstrate that final judgment must have *something* to do with works or with fulfilling the law. He adds this important observation about Rom 8: "In the center of the very chapter where Paul has declared that 'there is therefore now no condemnation for those who are in Christ Jesus,' he also writes, 'For if you live according to the flesh, you will die; but if by the Spirit you put to death the deeds of the body, you will live' (Romans 8:1, 13)" (185).

urges us to give ourselves entirely to the Spirit's agenda, to Christ coming to life within us and living out his desires for us and for the world through us.[16]

The cumulative evidence of Paul's writings challenges the oft-held assumption that Rom 10:9—"If you confess Jesus to be Lord with your mouth and trust in your heart that God raised him from the dead, you will be saved"—is the be-all and end-all statement about our part in embracing the deliverance God offers. Or, to put it more positively, Rom 10:9 has to be interpreted within the framework of Paul's whole testimony about what it means to put our trust in Jesus and to claim Jesus with our lips for these acts of trusting and confessing to be effective. If our theology does not have room for the statements of Paul examined in this and preceding sections, it might be prudent to reexamine this theology, resisting the temptation to soft-pedal, domesticate, or overlook these texts entirely because they don't fit with our theology of "how to get saved."[17]

---

16. Although quite supportive of the view that God *does* expect changed lives, Bird would probably not be happy with this view of justification because, in his estimation, "it shifts the material cause of eschatological justification from Christology to pneumatology. On such a perspective Paul differs from Judaism not by asserting that a negative outcome at the future judgment has been averted by Christ, but departs only by his belief that Christians are uniquely powered to meet its requirements" (*Saving Righteousness*, 173). I think it a gain, however, to give proper weight to the oft-neglected third person of the Trinity in this process, especially when Paul himself gives such weight to the same (as in Gal 3:14; 5:5-6). In the one passage in 1 Corinthians in which Paul uses the verb *dikaioō*, he uses it in connection with the work both of Christ *and* of the Spirit: "You were washed; you were made holy; you were justified in the name of the Lord Jesus Christ and in the Spirit of our God" (1 Cor 6:11). It is therefore certainly not un-Pauline to assign to the Spirit some role, at the very least, in justification. Gottlob Schenk also observes that, in Gal 3:2, 5, "very similar expressions are used for the reception of the Spirit as for justification by faith in R[om]. 3:28" ("*Dikē*, etc.," in *Theological Dictionary of the New Testament*, ed. Gerhard Kittel, trans. G. W. Bromiley [Grand Rapids: Eerdmans, 1964], 2:208), going so far as to conclude that "it is only pneumatology which fulfills the work of justification" (209). Thus I would plead with Wright in a solidly trinitarian fashion: "When, by clear implication, I am charged with encouraging believers to put their trust in someone or something 'other than the crucified and resurrected Savior,' I want to plead guilty ... that I trust in the Holy Spirit" (*Justification*, 188). At the same time, Christ's place is not in fact diminished, since the work of the Holy Spirit is to bring into being the mystery of Christ coming alive within us and living through us (see Gal 2:19-20; 4:19). Paul is even Christocentric when speaking of the work of the Spirit and the transformation of the believer.

17. N. T. Wright (*Justification*, 31) draws a helpful analogy between theologies of Paul and jigsaw puzzles, noting that many interpreters (including the theologians in the pews) leave a good number of pieces in the box or sweep them off the table onto the floor and then try to force the remaining pieces together into some kind of picture.

Paul's gospel, however, remains *good* news: it is the message about how God has undertaken to work out our transformation. It is about God's provision for our transformation so that by means of his gifts we might become righteous and thus be approved at the Last Judgment *without* God himself ceasing to be just. It is indeed about how "God demonstrates himself to be just while at the same time also making those who have put their trust in Jesus righteous themselves" (Rom 3:26).

What Does "Justification" Involve for Paul?

What does it mean to say that "God justifies the ungodly" (Rom 4:4)?[18] Since our transformation is such a prominent facet of Paul's good news, and since "God shows no partiality" in the judgment, "justification" in its fullness must involve more than a legal ruling whereby the guilty are, contrary to the facts of the case, declared innocent because God accepted the punishment of an innocent man in our place. In legal contexts this group of words does carry the sense of "vindication" or "acquittal," thus a verdict in favor of the party in question. Paul certainly uses words from this group in the context of legal language, particularly in Rom 2–3. But he does not *only* use the word when describing the courtroom scene of the Last Judgment, and neither are there good indications that we should read this context into *every* appearance of the words "justification," "justify," "just," or "justice [righteousness]" in Paul.

A person is considered to be "just" (*dikaios*) in the ancient world insofar as that person "upholds the customs and norms of [acceptable]

---

18. The question has spawned an overwhelmingly vast amount of scholarly and popular works. For a recent and helpful overview of the spectrum of answers, see James K. Beilby and Paul R. Eddy, eds., *Justification: Five Views* (Downers Grove, IL: InterVarsity Press, 2011). Some important, recent statements on the topic from different perspectives include Wright, *Justification*; Bird, *Saving Righteousness*; Mark A. Seifrid, *Christ Our Righteousness* (Downers Grove, IL: InterVarsity Press, 2000); and Michael J. Gorman, *Inhabiting the Cruciform God* (Grand Rapids: Eerdmans, 2009).

behavior" as those are defined by his or her society.[19] A person was "just" insofar as he or she lived in line with an established norm. In the NT, which is very much in line with usage in the Greek OT (the Septuagint), the *dikaios* ("just person") is contrasted with the sinner (Matt 9:13; Mark 2:17; Luke 5:32; 15:7; Rom 5:19), the unjust person (Matt 5:45; Acts 24:15), the disobedient person (Luke 1:17), the ungodly (Rom 5:6–7; 1 Tim 1:9; 1 Pet 4:18), the lawless person (Matt 13:41; 1 Tim 1:9), the wicked person (Matt 13:49), and the play-actor (Matt 23:28; Luke 20:20). From this picture of what he or she is *not*, the *dikaios* is clearly one who fulfills God's just requirements in a manner showing mindfulness of his or her duty toward God and thus what is owed to others on account of God. He or she is a person whose attitudes and practices please God for having done what God wished for him or her to do and for having done it in a spirit of reverence for God.[20]

The related noun "justice" or "righteousness" (*diakiosynē*) is similarly defined as "uprightness as determined by divine/legal standards."[21] The word speaks of lining up positively with an existing norm or set of standards, whether this be "the civil virtue of observance of law and fulfillment of duty" or "observance of the commandments."[22] In both Hellenistic Jewish and early Christian authors it is set against *anomia*

19. Thus Walter Bauer, Frederick Danker, et al., *A Greek-English Lexicon of the New Testament and Other Early Christian Literature*, 3rd ed. (Chicago: University of Chicago Press, 2000), 246, col. 1; Ceslaus Spicq, "*dikaios*, etc.," in *Theological Lexicon of the New Testament*, trans. James D. Ernest (Peabody, MA: Hendrickson, 1994), 1:322–25; Schrenk, "*Dikē*, etc.," in *Theological Dictionary of the New Testament*, 2:182, 185, 189–90, 192, 196. In Hellenistic Jewish writings, the word commonly and quite naturally refers to the person who obeys God's law, the Torah (as in Josephus, *Ag. Ap.* 2.293; *Ant.* 6.165; 8.208).
20. Spicq, "*dikaios*, etc.," 324.
21. Bauer, Danker, et al., *Greek-English Lexicon*, 248, col. 2. Wright fights vigorously against allowing the word to bear this rather standard meaning, as if the law court image determines every Pauline usage of this word and related terms, or as if the specialized meanings that Wright promotes as Paul's own (e.g., "membership in God's true family," as in *Justification*, 121, 134) would trump the normal usage of this word in the Graeco-Roman context for Paul's hearers (let alone for Paul himself). Despite Wright's protests to the contrary (*Justification*, 230) Paul's usage of the term in Rom 6:16–20 suggests that *dikaiosynē* must bear its principal meaning of "justice" or "righteousness" as an enacted moral quality so that it may stand as a more suitable antithesis to "sin" in 6:16 and 6:20.
22. Schrenk, "*Dikē*, etc.," 192, 194.

("lawlessness") and *hamartia* ("sin") as their antonym.[23] When thinking about "justification" it is vitally important to observe that Paul does not only speak of "acquittal" or "vindication" (*dikaiōsis*) as God's goal for us in Jesus or our goal in entrusting ourselves to Jesus; he also speaks of "righteousness" (*dikaiosynē*) as the goal of our hope and God's actions. These two terms are not identical: *dikaiōsis* speaks of the result of the legal action on behalf of believers; *dikaiosynē* names the ethical virtue of righteousness, the result of living in line with a set of ethical norms, here particularly the standards that God holds for the behavior of God's creatures. The ethical virtue of righteousness, of course, can provide the basis for a legal verdict. Sometimes our English translations get these terms confused, translating *both* terms as "justification."[24] This is not due to some ambiguity or overlap in the usage of the Greek terms. It is due rather to the theological convictions, conscious or otherwise, of translators who are reluctant to admit that Paul really expects God to transform us into righteous people, people who do what is just in God's sight or otherwise live in conformity with God's standards.[25]

We come at last then to the consideration of the primary verb that belongs to this word group, *dikaioō*. This verb is commonly used in legal contexts in the sense of declaring that a person is just in regard

---

23. In the non-Pauline writings of the NT, *dikaiosynē* "is almost always used in the NT for the right conduct of man which follows the will of God and is pleasing to Him, for rectitude of life before God, for uprightness before His judgment." If anything distinguishes this usage from the larger Greek world it is in the relationship with God that is the context for righteousness and in that the knowledge of what is "right conduct" comes through divine revelation (Schrenk, "*Dikē*, etc.," 198).

24. This error can be observed, for example, in the NRSV of Rom 5:21; 2 Cor 3:9; Gal 2:21.

25. I find something of this problem in Mark Seifrid's statement that "Paul often uses the nouns *dikaiosunē* and *dikaiōsis* in speaking of the triumph of God or the new creation that issues from it. ... Nowhere in the Pauline literature does 'righteousness' appear as a virtue which may be acquired as it does in Josephus or other Hellenistic authors" ("Paul's Use," 54). Seifrid makes an unwarranted leap in his word study. His first sentence treats the noun *dikaio-synē* as an abbreviation for the specific phrase *dikaiosynē theou*, "the righteousness of God." In regard to this phrase his observation holds true. This would *not*, however, apply to *dikaiosynē* without the modifier *theou* (i.e., "of God"). It is also highly questionable that we should expect Paul to use a very common word like *dikaiosynē* to mean something that would not at least overlap with its common, ethical meaning "in Josephus or other Hellenistic authors" (to which we could add "non-Pauline" NT uses), that is, with the meaning it has in *normal* Greek usage. Contrast Schrenk ("*Dikē*, etc.," 195–96), where this distinction between *dikaiosynē theou* and *dikaiosynē* as the characteristic of human beings committed to "the observance of the will of God which is well-pleasing to Him" is well drawn.

to the cause that has been brought before the court.[26] This is especially true when the goal of the justifying action is "acquittal" or "vindication" (*dikaiōsis*). When the goal of the justifying action is, however, also "righteousness" (*dikaiosynē*), that justifying action carries the causative sense typical of verbs formed by joining a noun or adjective to the -oō morpheme, thus "to make" or "to cause someone to *be* just" in the sense of "bring someone or something in line with a standard." "Justification" in this sense entails realignment.[27] It involves the process by which God makes the Christ follower just, transforming him or her into a person who exhibits *dikaiosynē*.

Justification is, in the legal or forensic sense, the recognition by God before all at the Last Judgment that one has lived in line with God's righteous standards.[28] But as Paul describes the transformation effected by the power of God within believers, he names another action of "justification" at work as God brings *us* in line with God's standards of righteousness by lining us up with Christ, even bringing Christ, the One who is perfectly aligned with God's righteousness, to life within us. Because of this transformation, the final verdict of acquittal or

26. It can also mean "enforce justice" in the sense of "execute punishment," though this meaning is almost unattested in the Septuagint and NT (see Schrenk, "*Dikē*, etc.," 223; Seifrid, "Paul's Use," 45–50).

27. "Since Paul views God's justifying action in close connection with the power of Christ's resurrection, there is sometimes no clear distinction between the justifying action of acquittal and the gift of new life through the Holy Spirit as God's activity in promoting uprightness in believers" (Bauer, Danker, et al., *Greek-English Lexicon*, 249, 2.b.β). This sense of the word "justification" survives in modern English usage in the context of typing and word processing. I recall how, in high school and college, teachers would specify whether they wanted papers turned in with "left justification," indicating that they wanted only the words on the left margin to line up, or "full justification," indicating that they wanted the words on both margins to line up (a possibility introduced with the most primitive generation of word processors). Justification means "being lined up with some standard," thus being "set right" in regard to that particular standard.

28. I find myself here, I believe, in substantial agreement with the statement on justification in Wright, *Justification*, 251: "The present verdict gives the *assurance that* the future verdict will match it; the Spirit gives the *power through which* that future verdict, when given, will be seen to be in accordance with the life that the believer has then lived." The life lived by the Christian between coming to trust in Jesus and his or her death certainly matters to Paul (Bird, *Saving Righteousness*, 159; Wright, *Justification*, 191; Gathercole, "A Law unto Themselves," 48). This does not mean that final judgment is ultimately *performance*-based since, while "God indeed requires works as the basis for *final* justification," it is nevertheless God himself who "produces in the believer through the Spirit the works he requires" (N. T. Wright, *Paul: In Fresh Perspective* [Minneapolis: Fortress, 2006], 148; see also Bird, *Saving Righteousness*, 176).

approbation (*dikaiōsis*) reflects the truth of the life lived by the power of the Spirit that God provides to those who are in Christ.[29]

Some theologians will experience discomfort, perhaps even pique, at the nestling of the kind of process usually referred to as "sanctification" *within*, and as essential to, "justification." In keeping with the commitment of the Reformation church to be *semper reformanda*, however, it is necessary to consider at least *whether* we have separated asunder what Paul understood to be joined more integrally and thereby lost sight of important elements of Paul's understanding of God's justifying action on behalf of believers, not to mention the relationship between initial and final justification.[30]

Attaining righteousness and making full use of the God-given means for becoming righteous are of great concern for Paul. This was also apparently something of great concern to his converts in Galatia. It was their desire to attain this goal that led at least some of them to think seriously about adopting a Torah-observant lifestyle at the urging of some Jewish–Christian teachers who made their way into Paul's mission territory. Nowhere in Galatians does Paul oppose their goal of attaining righteousness—only the means by which they are thinking to attain it, instead urging them to make use of the gift of the Holy Spirit as the means to that end. It is significant that Paul never says "stop worrying about attaining righteousness," but rather describes how God has already provided them with what they need to attain that goal.

---

29. Charles Talbert (*Romans* [Macon, GA: Smyth & Helwys, 2002], 82) expresses the difference between "justification by works" and "justification on the basis of works" with helpful precision: "The apparent contradiction between Paul's claim that no one is justified by (*ek*) works and the contention in this text [viz., Rom 2:1–11] that all are judged on the basis of (*kata; dia*) their works may be resolved if one notes the prepositions used by the apostle in the two statements. On the one hand, when Paul said 'no one will be justified by works of law' (Rom 3:20; Gal 2:16), his language was *ex ergon nomou*. The *ek* expressed instrumentality, not evidential basis. So Paul was saying that the means of justification is not works of law. On the other hand, when he said those who do the law will be justified or that one will be judged on the basis of his/her deeds (Rom 2:7, 12, 13; cf. Rom 2:10; 1 Cor 4:3–5; 2 Cor 5:10), Paul spoke about the basis of final justification. It is deeds done in the body."

30. See also Schrenk (*Dikē*, etc.," 209): "The justifying action of God ... is always teleological. ... Thus, without any sense of difficulty or contradiction, the thought of pardoning and forensic righteousness passes over into that of righteousness as the living power which overcomes sin. The righteousness which is given commits the believer to the living power of *dikaiosunē*." For a similar articulation of a more holistic understanding of justification see Talbert, *Romans*, 179–80.

> Having begun with the Spirit, are you finishing with the flesh? (Gal 3:3)

> I don't set aside God's grace, for if righteousness (*dikaiosynē*) could be attained through Torah, then Christ died for nothing. (Gal 2:21)

> If a law that was able to make people alive had been given, then righteousness (*dikaiosynē*) would indeed be attained on the basis of the Torah. (Gal 3:21)

The assumption behind particularly the last two statements is that attaining righteousness *is* in fact the goal toward which Paul and his Galatian converts are rightly pressing. The point at issue in Galatians concerns the *means* to this end—the Torah as an external set of standards and practices to be adopted, or the Spirit as an internal norm to guide and to shape. Paul affirms both the goal and the Spirit as the means to attain it later in this same letter: "By the Spirit we await the hoped-for righteousness (*dikaiosynē*) on the basis of trust, for in Christ Jesus neither circumcision nor lack of circumcision is of any effect, but rather committed trust [*pistis*, "faith"] working through love" (Gal 5:5–6).

"Faith putting itself to work through love"—*this* is what Paul says matters to God rather than one's status as a Jew or Gentile. This is what brings one into line with God's standards[31] and thus fulfills God's standards for righteousness—not living as a Jew, putting into practice what Paul calls "the works of the law" or "the works of Torah." Paul is not against "good works." On the contrary, he urges his converts to make

---

31. Wright reduces "the hope of *dikaiosynē*" in Gal 5:5–6 to "the verdict that is still eagerly awaited" (*Justification*, 144), which is again not to allow Paul to use *dikaiosynē* in its common and natural sense of the moral quality manifested in a particular set of commitments and practices (that will, incidentally, be recognized as "just" at the Last Judgment). This is indeed the meaning suggested by 5:6, where "faith putting itself to work through love" is clearly suggestive of attitudes and practices that God will look upon with favor as manifesting alignment with God's standards of righteousness—since love in action is what fulfills God's law and the law of the Messiah (Gal 5:13–14; 6:2).

faith effective through works that show other-centered and God-centered love, works that move us in the opposite direction of "works of the flesh."[32]

Taken out of context, some of Paul's expressions may *seem* to oppose faith to works of any kind. Romans 4:4–5 might be taken as a case in point: "Now to one who works, wages are not reckoned as a gift but as something due. But to one who without works trusts him who justifies the ungodly, such faith is reckoned as righteousness" (Rom 4:4–5 NRSV). When we read such passages in their fuller context, however, it becomes clear that he consistently has in view those "works" that set apart the Jew from the Gentile on the assumption that such ethnic categories matter to God on this side of Christ's coming. In this instance, the preceding paragraph (Rom 3:27–30) makes clear that Paul is chiefly concerned with those works that identify a person as a member of ethnic Israel, as if God were "the God of the Jews only" and not also "God of the Gentiles."[33] Similarly, the following paragraph reaffirms the identification of "works" here purely with marks of ethnic identity like circumcision (4:11–13).

Fulfilling God's law through living in alignment with God's righteousness and righteous demands still matters very much to Paul.

---

32. In this way, transformation actualized shows the quality of the faith that the individual possesses—and it is the faith that results in transformation of character and life that saves. On this point see Bird, *Saving Righteousness*, 178: "The works that are performed in-Christ as empowered by the Spirit demonstrate the integrity of the faith that the believer professes. ... Works as christologically conceived, pneumatically empowered, and divinely endowed are necessary for salvation in so far as they reveal the character of authentic faith expressed in the form of obedience, love, faithfulness, righteousness and holiness."

33. Wright (*Justification*, 52–53) correctly stresses the relationship of 3:27–28 to 3:29–30, which are joined by a Greek conjunction meaning "or." Thus the latter verses guide the interpretation of the former. For Paul, if the truth of Rom 3:28 is not admitted, then God will look like the God of only Jews rather than the God of all people (3:29). The "works of the law" in question are therefore not the "good works" that Protestants love to hate, but the works that set Jews apart from Gentiles, a social boundary that no longer has positive value since the coming of faith.

Circumcision is nothing and lack of circumcision is nothing, but keeping God's commandments [is what matters]. (1 Cor 7:19)[34]

You were called to freedom, brothers and sisters, only not freedom as an opportunity for the flesh—rather, through love, become slaves one to another. For the entire Torah has been fulfilled in a single word, in the command "You will love your neighbor as yourself." (Gal 5:13–14)

Owe no one anything, except to love one another; for the one who loves another has fulfilled the law. The commandments, "You shall not commit adultery; You shall not murder; You shall not steal; You shall not covet"; and any other commandment, are summed up in this word, "Love your neighbor as yourself." Love does no wrong to a neighbor; therefore, love is the fulfilling of the law. (Rom 13:8–10 NRSV)

"Doing" the Torah is no longer the path to aligning oneself with God's righteousness and thus arriving at final justification. Nevertheless, those who belong to Jesus and allow the Spirit to direct them *fulfill* the just requirements of the Torah. Indeed, on three occasions in Romans— one of the later letters that we have from Paul's hand and therefore one written from a more mature perspective on his own work—Paul summarizes the purpose of his mission as nurturing "the obedience that comes from faith" among his converts (Rom 1:6; 16:25–26), especially "the obedience of the Gentiles" in response to the message about God's provision for deliverance from wrath (Rom 15:18).

The righteousness of which we are speaking is not what Paul censures as "a righteousness of our own" (see Rom 10:3; Phil 3:9). It is rather

---

34. Klyne Snodgrass ("Justification by Grace," 72–93, 78) uses this verse, in conjunction with the similar formulaic statement in Gal 5:6, as a summary of what really matters for Paul and what he understood the gospel to accomplish in the lives of the faithful: "Being a new creation for Paul meant a life of faith working through love, and outside the context of the debate over 'works righteousness,' this could even be described as a life of keeping the commandments of God."

the "righteousness that comes from God" since it is the product of God's Spirit at work within us, bringing Christ to life within and through us.[35] But it is righteousness, as reflected in a mind, will, and record of action that shows a person to think, seek, and do what is pleasing in God's sight since he or she moves in alignment with God's own Spirit.

Combined with God's forgiveness of our sins and shortcomings, it is this positive righteousness that will allow a person to stand "blameless" in God's presence—something for which Paul prays repeatedly (1 Cor 1:8–9; Eph 1:4; Col 1:21–23; 1 Thess 3:13; 5:23). The connection is most explicit in his prayer for his friends in Philippi:

> I pray this—that your love may abound still more and more accompanied by knowledge and all discernment in order that you may be able to tell what really makes a difference, in order that you may be pure and blameless until the day of Christ, being full (*peplērōmenoi*) of the fruit of righteousness, the fruit that comes through Jesus Christ for God's glory and praise. (Phil 1:9-11)

Growth in awareness and discernment (and, implicitly, in practice, based on what one has discerned) will lead them into lives of righteousness, a stream of practices and deeds that can be called "a harvest of righteousness" (Phil 1:11 NRSV). This remains a work of God, for it is *God* who sowed this crop in the soil that was their lives. It is the fruition of the seed of receiving Christ, forgiveness, a changed relationship with God, and an invitation to a new and glorious destiny. It is the result of the Spirit's work in bringing the seed to fructification. Producing this crop is at the very least the antecedent of standing "pure and blameless" in the day of Christ; it might be read here as the *basis* for the same.[36] Read in the context of the famous verse that precedes this (Phil 1:6), this

---

35. This is rarely lost to view. Catholic scholar Ceslaus Spicq, for example, affirms concerning the disciple's growth into righteousness that "everything depends on the connection with Christ" ("*dikaios*, etc.," 325n26).

36. The issue here concerns how to understand the relationship of the action expressed by the adverbial participle *peplērōmenoi*, which can be understood as naming a (completed) condition or a cause. I would understand the latter to be the more likely, given that "standing blameless" is the purpose for which the believers are said to exercise their God-given knowledge and discernment.

crop of righteousness marks God's bringing to completion the good work that God began in us. It is for *this* that God has been cultivating us from the beginning.

The many passages from Paul that we have been exploring push us in the direction of a view of justification in which God *brings into being* within us the righteousness that Christ exhibited, changing us to become more like him, indeed inviting us to become vessels through which Christ's righteousness continues to express itself in real, effective ways in the communities and world around us. This process begins with and depends fully upon Christ's own act of obedience, but the end result is that we become obedient to God as well. Paul writes, "For just as the many were made sinners through one man's act of disobedience, so also the many will be made righteous through the obedience of the one man" (Rom 5:19). Adam and Jesus emerge as two paradigms for humanity, and Paul presents them as completely parallel. All people share in the consequences of Adam's transgression not only because of his historic transgression, but because all people born of this conceptual common ancestor sin just as he did: "Therefore, just as sin entered the cosmos through one person and death entered through sin, and just as death came upon all people, *since all sinned ...* " (Rom 5:12, a sentence that Paul himself doesn't complete). Now Christ's act of obedience opens afresh the possibility of obedience for those in whom Christ's Spirit comes to dwell. Justification is not a matter of escaping deserved judgment because Christ's innocence is somehow projected onto us on the Day of Judgment. It is a process in which God invests himself fully in our transformation and calls us to respond to God's work with equal investment. And we can even now be confident of the successful outcome of this process because "God is the one working in and among [us] both to desire and to labor on behalf of what pleases him" (Phil 2:13).

N. T. Wright would fault me on this point for trying to make the concept of justification include too much. He complains that the idea

> has regularly been made to do duty for *the entire picture of God's reconciling action toward the human race*, covering everything from God's free love and grace, through the sending of the son to die and rise again for sinners, through

the preaching of the gospel, the work of the Spirit, the
arousal of faith in human hearts and minds, the development of Christian character and conduct, the assurance
of ultimate salvation, and the safe passage through final
judgment to that destination.[37]

He would prefer to restrict the term to "*one specific aspect of* or *moment
within* that sequence of thought."[38] He offers an analogy for what has
gone wrong in the application of the language of "justification" in the
image of a person who, correctly discerning that the steering wheel is
an essential component of an automobile, refers to the whole car as the
steering wheel.

I would suggest, however, that if we are to understand justification
from Paul's point of view it ought not to be likened to *any* part of the car
itself. Wright would agree that justification has to do with something
that happens now in Christ and happens eschatologically at the judgment. It would be truer to Paul's thought to think of justification, then,
as the destination toward which we are driving—or, better, toward
which we are being chauffeured by the Spirit—the destination at which
we would surely arrive if we just stopped grabbing the wheel ourselves,
or, worse, jumping out of the car and making the Spirit take detours
to try to find us again and coax us back into the vehicle. To anticipate
the objection that justification is also a present reality, let us imagine our chauffeur, the Spirit, arriving to meet us with a sign reading
"Justification" and including an image of Christ crucified on the placard
(cf. Gal 3:1–5). The question of faith becomes this: do we trust this Jesus
enough to get in the car with this Spirit and thus trust to arrive also at
the final destination by the means he has provided?

---

37. Ibid., 86. That Wright would also thus criticize Luther (see Seifrid, "Paul's Use," 71), however, gives me considerable solace.
38. Wright, *Justification*, 87.

ONCE SAVED, ALWAYS SAVED — BUT WHEN "SAVED"? SALVATION AS A "WORK IN PROCESS"

The language of "being saved" often has a very specific meaning in modern usage, particularly among evangelical Christians. The phrase generally names the reality of encountering Jesus and receiving him as Lord, entering into a relationship with him, putting one's trust in him, and being thus invited into a living relationship with him. Paul also speaks of these realities. For example, Paul speaks about Christians as already "saved" in his words to the Christians in Ephesus: "You have been saved by grace through faith" (Eph 2:8). In his advice to Titus he writes, "When the goodness and beneficence of God, our Savior, manifested itself, he delivered/saved us (not on the grounds of works we performed in righteousness, but in accordance with his mercy) through the washing of a new beginning ('regeneration') and through renewal effected by the Holy Spirit" (Titus 3:4–5).[39] It is important to note, however, that he does not restrict his usage of "salvation" language to these experiences. Instead the language of "salvation" and "being saved" is part of a much larger divine drama into which we are swept up.

Thus while Paul will speak of our *having been* saved in a sense, many of Paul's statements indicate that there is another sense in which salvation is still *out there* in front of us as something toward which to keep pressing on, a sense in which we are still in the process of experiencing the deliverance that God has prepared for us. Paul says that "the word about the cross ... is, to those who are being saved, the power of God," as opposed to "those who are perishing," to whom it is "foolishness" (1 Cor 1:18).[40] People find themselves in one of two processes ("being saved" or "perishing") during their lifetime depending on their response to the gospel—but just as those who reject the message about

---

39. The authorship of the Pastoral Letters (1 & 2 Timothy, Titus) is even more disputed than that of Ephesians and Colossians. While Luke Timothy Johnson has crafted a strong case in favor of the authenticity of 2 Timothy (*The First and Second Letters to Timothy*, Yale Anchor Bible Commentaries [New Haven, CT: Yale University Press, 2001]), one is well advised to be cautious about using 1 Timothy and Titus as documents from "the historical Paul." For a survey of the arguments see deSilva, *Introduction to the New Testament*, 733–48.

40. The two groups—"those who are being delivered" and "those who are perishing"—are described using present participles in Greek, the present tense of the participle indicating here individuals in the thick of a process or of an action.

the deliverance God has made possible through Christ are "on their way out," so those who have responded openly and gratefully are still in the process of experiencing that deliverance. Just as "those who are in the process of perishing" have not yet perished, so "those who are in the process of being saved" have not yet anchored in their eternal harbor.

This perspective comes out even more clearly—perhaps surprisingly—in Romans itself. For Paul, salvation or deliverance is what happens at the end of the journey. It is rooted in what God has already done for us; it is drawing closer every day; but it is certainly not simply *behind* us:

> You know what time it is, how it is now the moment for you
> to wake from sleep. For *salvation is nearer to us now than*
> *when we became believers*; the night is far gone, the day is
> near. Let us then lay aside the works of darkness and put
> on the armor of light; let us live honorably as in the day,
> not in reveling and drunkenness, not in debauchery and
> licentiousness, not in quarreling and jealousy. Instead,
> put on the Lord Jesus Christ, and make no provision for
> the flesh, to gratify its desires. (Rom 13:11–14 NRSV)

Two important points emerge from this passage. First, "salvation" remains something that lies ahead of Paul and his audience; second, an ethical response is necessitated by the point at which believers find themselves in God's timeline (i.e., with the day approaching closer and closer). If we look forward to deliverance ("salvation") on the day of judgment, or the day of Christ's visitation, the light of *that* day must illumine all our steps today, tomorrow, and all our days.

Since I am swimming against some strong theological currents, I want to float another text from Romans. Paul celebrates God's astounding generosity (God's "grace") being displayed in God's giving his best gift (reconciliation through the death of his Son) to those who are furthest from deserving such kindness (those who have made themselves God's enemies through their disobedience and rebellion). In light of this:

> How much more surely, now that we are brought back
> in line with God's righteous standards by Jesus' blood,
> will we be saved through him from wrath? For if, while

> we were still enemies, we were reconciled to God through
> his son's death, how much more surely, now that we are
> reconciled, will we be saved by his life? (Rom 5:9-10)

It is important to notice here that, in Romans at least, "being justified" (the more typical way of rendering in English what I have translated more fully as "brought back in line with God's righteous standards") is not yet the same thing as being "saved"; similarly, being reconciled to God is not the same as being "saved." Moreover, being "saved" is clearly an experience for which Paul looks to the future. He understands his present experience of reconciliation with God and realignment with God's righteousness ("being justified") as assurance of the future experience, but it nonetheless remains future rather than already possessed and experienced (i.e., something "in one's pocket").

Because of this, Paul can urge his friends in Philippi to "keep working out your deliverance/salvation with fear and trembling, for God is the one working in/among you both to desire and to work on behalf of what pleases him" (Phil 2:12-13). And with consummate humility he can say of himself that he has not yet "arrived":

> I want to know Christ and the power of his resurrection
> and the sharing of his sufferings by becoming like him
> in his death, if somehow I may attain the resurrection
> from the dead. *Not that I have already obtained this or have
> already reached the goal; but I press on to make it my own,
> because Christ Jesus has made me his own. Beloved, I do not
> consider that I have made it my own*; but this one thing I do:
> forgetting what lies behind and straining forward to what
> lies ahead, *I press on toward the goal* for the prize of the
> heavenly call of God in Christ Jesus. Let those of us then
> who are mature be of the same mind; and if you think differently about anything, this too God will reveal to you.
> (Phil 3:10-15 NRSV)

Allowing God's work within us to achieve its full effect, focusing our ambitions on becoming more and more like Jesus, particularly the heart for and commitment to God and others shown in his self-giving obedience unto death—if we heed Paul, these become our driving passions and agenda as we look forward to the completion of the deliverance God is providing for us.[41]

When Christians say that they are "saved" or ask others whether they are "saved" and then tell them how to "get saved" (admittedly a decreasing problem in many churches that are even more sadly forgetting how to evangelize at all), they foster a distorted view of this life. They speak and act as if the decisions and acts that carry eternal significance are all behind them and as if the present moment no longer mattered for eternity. John Donne, a 17th-century poet and Anglican priest, was much closer to Paul's gospel when he said that "upon every minute of this life depend millions of years in the next, and I shall be glorified eternally or eternally lost for my good or ill use of God's grace offered me this hour."[42] Such a thought can arouse some degree of anxiety. But once we get past this (since we move forward by trust), it also lends profound significance to each moment, to every encounter, every choice, every pursuit into which we throw ourselves, because these things truly matter for eternity. What we do between our profession of faith or the strange warming of our hearts or being "born again" (however we conceptualize the beginning of our faith journey) and the end of our lives is important in God's sight. What we do today, tomorrow, and the day after has everlasting significance.

A Great Gift Is a Great Responsibility

There remains yet one essential concept to address, the one that might be regarded as the most foundational in Paul's understanding of the "good news" that he has been commissioned to deliver, and that is the concept of grace. *Sola gratia* is one of the principal motifs of Reformation

---

41. Paul could integrate his convictions about being justified on the basis of faith and about his own experience of investment and effort in this venture since "at every point, he says, it is Christ working in me; it is God's grace which is with me; it is God energizing me to will what is good and to do it—and it is God who is pleased with the result" (Wright, *Justification*, 153). If we have a problem with this because it seems to cast "a shadow of doubt over 'justification by faith,'" the problem lies with our traditions and not with Paul.
42. John Donne, *The Sermons of John Donne*, ed. E. M. Simpson and G. R. Potter (Berkeley: University of California Press, 1953–1962), 3:514.

theology, and yet we often consider grace wholly as a *theologoumenon*, (that is, as a specialized term that takes its bearings primarily from Christian theology) and do not consider the implications of the fact that, at the time Paul formulated his teachings about God's grace, "grace" was a term very much at home in and informed by the social practices of patronage, friendship, and benefaction and by the social value of reciprocity as the ethic that infused those practices—a notion we will explore in more detail below.

Informed by this context, Paul's audiences would understand that God expected them not just to "receive" his gifts but to make the use of, and response to, his gifts that show an appropriate assessment of their value. Paul writes a sentence that never makes it into popular reductions of his gospel but that I believe is absolutely central: "[Christ] died on behalf of all in order that those who continue living might no longer live for themselves, but for the one who died on their behalf and was raised" (2 Cor 5:15). This is a purpose statement. Paul has framed it as one answer, at least, to the question "Why did Christ die for us?" The answer is stunning in the scope of its claim upon the disciple: he died for us so that we would live no longer for ourselves but for him.[43] Paul had in fact articulated something similar in Galatians, applying this conviction to himself in his statement about the results of encountering Christ's self-giving love and placing his trust in that relationship:

> I died to the Torah through the Torah in order that I might live to God. I was crucified together with Christ; it's no longer *me* living, but *Christ* living in me. The life I'm living

---

43. Wright reads 2 Corinthians 5:14–21 in the context of Paul's extensive defense of his apostleship in 2:14–6:13, which is surely correct, but this leads Wright to some incorrect conclusions about the limits on the meaning of this verse, namely that 2 Cor 5:15b is all about Paul living for Jesus and not a general statement that *all* indeed are bound now to live for the one who died and was raised on their behalf (*Justification*, 161). Second Corinthians 5:14b–15, however, should be read as Paul's statement of what he and his team have discerned to be the needful and appropriate response to the act of God in Christ, not just for their own response but indeed for the response of the "all" for whom Christ died. Such a reading honors the context of Paul's defense of his apostleship, but it is understood as the essential insight that drives Paul's mission—calling "all" to render to Christ his due by yielding their lives to him, even as Paul does (see Gal 2:19–20) and as Paul hopes his converts will do (see Gal 4:19).

> now in the flesh, I live in faith toward the Son of God who
> loved me and gave himself up for me. (Gal 2:19-20)

Paul refers to the Son of God who, out of love, "gave himself up" for Paul; Paul speaks now of giving up the remainder of his life so as to let that same Son of God live in and through him. Only a life given back shows the giver that we have properly valued his gift to us—his death on our behalf.

Such a response may seem extreme to us in our culture today, but the people who lived in the Greek and Roman world of the centuries shortly before and after Jesus had a much more robust notion of the connection between grace and response than we do.[44] The exchange of favors and gifts, and the formation of relationships involving such exchange, was the principal weave in the fabric of Greek and Roman society (so Seneca, *On Benefits*, 1.4.2). Because we are far removed from this social context, we tend to hear "the free gift" (a common translation of the Greek word *charisma*) to mean that there is no obligation on the recipient of such favor. Something is "free" if it costs us nothing. For Paul, however, "the free gift" speaks to the fact that the giving could not be coerced by any act of our own, as suggested also by Paul's rhetorical question, "Who has ever given to God, that God should repay them?" (Rom 11:35 NIV). The *giving* is free and uncoerced, but the *receiving* creates a relationship of obligation. In Paul's context, gifts and favors (to *be* such at all) were indeed "freely" *given* on the basis of the giver's generosity and motivation, but—and this is the essential point for us—a gift or favor received meant an obligation on the part of the recipient toward the giver. "Reciprocity," making an appropriate return for a gift given or a favor done, was firmly hardwired into their social and ethical consciousness.

This has profound implications for how we think about grace, since the language of grace such as Paul used (the Greek word *charis*) was at home principally in the setting of social relationships of reciprocity. It is particularly significant that the single Greek word *charis* can carry

---

44. A fuller introduction to this cultural background and its relevance for New Testament interpretation can be found in David A. deSilva, *Honor, Patronage, Kinship & Purity: Unlocking New Testament Culture* (Downers Grove, IL: InterVarsity Press, 2000), 95-156.

three distinct senses depending on the context. It can mean the disposition to show favor (hence, "grace"); it can be used to denote the gift given or favor done; and it can denote the response of gratitude made by the recipient of favors. This trinity of meanings suggests implicitly what many moralists from the Greek and Roman cultures stated explicitly: grace must be met with grace, favor must always give birth to favor (cf. Sophocles, *Ajax*, 522), gift must always be met with gratitude. The person who accepted a benefaction in the ancient world simultaneously accepted the obligation to show gratitude. In Seneca's words (*Ben.*, 2.25.3), "the person who intends to be grateful, immediately while receiving, should turn his or her thought to repaying."[45]

This point is well illustrated by a common motif in ancient art and a Roman philosopher's interpretation of that motif. I am referring here to the image of the three "Graces," three goddesses dancing hand-in-hand in a circle. Seneca interprets this image thus: there are three graces, since "there is one for bestowing a benefit, one for receiving it, and a third for returning it." They dance hand-in-hand because "a benefit passing in its course from hand to hand returns nevertheless to the giver; the beauty of the whole is destroyed if the course is anywhere broken, and it has most beauty if it is continuous and maintains an uninterrupted succession" (*Ben.*, 1.3.2–5). There ought not to be such a thing as an isolated act of "grace." An act of favor initiates a circle dance in which the recipients of favor must "return the favor," that is, give again to the giver (both in terms of a generous disposition and in terms of some gift, whether material or otherwise). Only a gift requited is a gift well and nobly received. Depicting the facets of the grace relationship as goddesses also communicated the sanctity of the relationship. Showing gratitude was considered a sacred obligation, while ingratitude was ranked alongside sacrilege (Dio, *Rhod.*, 37). As Seneca would sum it up: "to fail to return gratitude is a disgrace, and the whole world counts it as such" (*Ben.*, 3.1.1).

This fundamental cultural background is of great help for understanding the connection between grace and discipleship, between theology

---

45. Translation adapted from Seneca, *Moral Essays, Volume III* (trans. John W. Basore; LCL; Cambridge: Harvard University Press, 1928).

and ethics, throughout the NT. God's grace is an initiating act that creates a relationship and calls forth a proportional response. While we can never repay God or equal his grace, we are nevertheless provoked by God's generosity to live like people who can never give enough back to God, who can never reach a point where they can say "I've given back to God as God has given to me; I can start living for myself again now."

When we ask, "What is necessary for me to be saved?" we are not asking the right question. We should be asking instead, "Since Jesus gave his life *for me* and brought me the gifts of a fresh start with God and the Spirit of God to dwell within me, what is it right for me to do *for him* in return?" Or, "Where can I reasonably draw the line between living for him and living to serve my own interests and desires, since he, in his generous kindness, did not draw such lines?" We move from a minimalist question to a maximalist question—which only seems fair if we really believe that God gave his *all* to provide us with a way out and a way back, rather than giving the minimum that was necessary. This approach to the question of salvation, it seems to me, is really the one that resonates with the heart of the Paul who wrote the words found in 2 Cor 5:15 and Gal 2:19–20, with which this section began.

To those who might balk at the idea of a response to God's grace being a *necessary* corollary of our receiving God's grace, I would point out that Paul is not afraid to put our obligation to God even less delicately when his converts are behaving less than graciously: "You were purchased with a price, so bring honor to God with your body" (1 Cor 6:20). Redemption was an act of generous kindness—of grace—but being ransomed carries obligations toward the ransomer, if we appreciate the freedom that was purchased for us and the cost of our ransom. If freedom from sin and the gift of the Spirit that is able to work transformation within us were gained for us by Jesus' giving of himself over to death on our behalf, we are *not* ethically free to neglect this freedom and this gift in any of its aspects. Something that cost so much *must* be valued and made use of appropriately.

What is Jesus' death worth to you? Is his death for you worth living the rest of your life for him, his way, and not living the rest of your life for yourself, your way? As Paul succinctly put it, "Christ died for all in order that those who continued to live might live no longer for themselves but for the one who died and was raised on their behalf" (2 Cor 5:15). What if "saving faith" is such a life-altering, life-orienting trust, one that comes only from the proper valuing of what Christ has done on our behalf ("proper" being measured by the simple question, "Are we giving back to Jesus as he gave to us?")? As Isaac Watts put it in the closing couplet of the famous hymn "When I Survey the Wondrous Cross":

> Love so amazing, so divine,
> Demands my soul, my life, my all.

I do not believe that Paul would have Christians think about "justification" apart from verses like 2 Cor 5:15, for in Paul's view, giving our lives over to the one who gave his life for us is the fundamentally *just* response. Indeed it is as we give our lives over to Christ to live through us, turning away from our self-driven agendas and our self-directed goals and responses to situations, giving ourselves to Spirit-driven and Spirit-directed agendas and actions, that we *become* people who desire and do what is just in God's sight. We might begin to think of an economy in which God's act of generosity in Christ, Jesus' giving of himself for us, provokes a grateful response in us. Lifted up and impelled by this gratitude—something that is not our own doing, but a reaction to God's generosity, God's grace—we move into a new kind of life, not merely living for Jesus but even stepping out of the way so that he can live through us, moving us like the mind moves the parts of its body. And thus by God's grace we are brought in line with God's righteous standards and desires; we are transformed into what a just God can affirm and acquit, all by God's initiative. I think this is very much *good* news.

CHAPTER 2

The Gospel Means the Transformation of the Individual: You Are Free to Become a New Person in Christ

If a pastor's priorities can be assessed in terms of the attention he or she gives to particular themes or topics in preaching, then it may be significant that Paul spends considerably less space writing about "justification" in terms of forgiveness and acceptance by God or in terms of acquittal at the Last Judgment than he does writing about the change that he believes God seeks to effect in the lives of believers in between their trusting Jesus and standing before him at the judgment. In this chapter we will look more closely at Paul's vision for how God is at work in the transformation of the person who trusts in Christ to bring him or her from a state of nonalignment with God's righteousness to a state of alignment with the same. We will also examine how Paul can conceive of this transformation as both a gift (an act of grace, such that our justification remains "by grace," Rom 3:24) and as a work of God (such that the righteousness for which the believer hopes remains "the righteousness from God based on trust" rather than "one's own righteousness," Phil 3:9). At every point, Paul's vision for transformation greets the hearer as "good news."

You Were Freed for a Fresh Start with God

The starting point for our transformation is an astounding act of generosity on God's part, springing from the loving kindness that is as central to God's being as God's justice.

> While we were still weak, at the right time Christ died for the ungodly. Indeed, rarely will anyone die for a righteous person—though perhaps for a good person someone might actually dare to die. But God proves his love for us in that while we still were sinners Christ died for us. (Rom 5:6–8 NRSV)

As we observed in the closing section of the preceding chapter, relationships based on "grace" and reciprocity were fundamental to the social fabric of the Greek and Roman world. God's grace is "amazing" not because it is freely given, or given without being earned. That is inherent in any act of "grace" for it to be an act of grace rather than paying what is due. God's grace is amazing because God displays an extreme degree of generosity toward those who had displayed to God an extreme degree of disrespect and hostility. As Paul says in Romans 1:18–21, 24–25, 28, the very fact of our being ought to have generated a gratitude that made us live for God and walk in the ways that brought pleasure to the Creator. After we had already displayed such ingratitude as to live for ourselves and do what is ugly in God's sight, then God gives even more selflessly in the person of his Son Jesus Christ. He extends the gift of forgiveness and a clean start, a new opportunity to respond to God as God deserves and to be what God intended in our creation.

> In [Christ] we have redemption, the forgiveness of sins. … When you were dead in trespasses and the uncircumcision of your flesh, God made you alive together with him, when he forgave us all our trespasses, erasing the record that stood against us with its legal demands. He set this aside, nailing it to the cross. (Col 1:14; 2:13–14 NRSV)

> You who were once estranged and hostile in mind, do-
> ing evil deeds, he has now reconciled in his fleshly body
> through death, so as to present you holy and blameless
> before him—provided that you continue securely estab-
> lished and steadfast in the faith, without shifting from
> the hope promised by the gospel that you heard. (Col 1:21–
> 23 NRSV)

There are many theories about why it was necessary for Jesus to die, perhaps the most widely held involving Jesus suffering the punishment we deserve, or offering satisfaction to God's outraged justice.[1] But when one surveys the wondrous cross, it is not necessary to see a victim of God's anger; it is possible, perhaps even preferable, to see an expression of God's love, God's desire to draw people into this fresh start, this new beginning with God.

One of the key verses about the "atonement" comes, not surprisingly, again from Romans: "Since all have sinned and fall short of the glory of God; they are now justified by his grace as a gift, through the redemption that is in Christ Jesus, whom God put forward as *a sacrifice of atonement* by his blood, effective through faith" (Rom 3:23–25 NRSV). "A sacrifice of atonement" is one possible rendering of the Greek, but not the only one. Paul and the majority of Jews in the Mediterranean read their OT not just in Hebrew but also in a Greek translation (often referred to as the Septuagint). In fact the majority of Jews in this region *only* read their Scriptures in a Greek translation, since they had long since left their native language behind along with their native land. The Greek word Paul uses here is *hilastērion*, which is also used in the Greek translation of Exodus and Leviticus to denote the "mercy seat," the cover of the ark of the covenant, the place where God met humanity most intimately for reconciliation. Daniel Bailey has suggested that the verse be read thus: "God put forward his Son as a mercy seat," the new place

---

1. This is typically referred to as the "penal substitution" view of the atonement. An accessible primer on three of the major models of the atonement is James Beilby and Paul R. Eddy, eds., *The Nature of the Atonement: Four Views* (Downers Grove, IL: InterVarsity Press, 2006). (The fourth view is that no one view adequately captures the significance of Jesus' death.)

of reconciliation.[2] This is an attractive possibility in that it makes better sense of God's initiative in this act: in Jesus, and specifically in his death, God is extending to us a place to meet and come to terms.

However this particular word is rendered, God's initiative remains the most striking element in this passage. This is grace, this is God's generosity—not that we had to begin this journey of transformation by finding our way back to an offended God, but that God found his way to us. The terrible execution of Jesus—and whatever it is in God's economy we must never forget that it was also an act of oppressive brutality by a political regime protecting itself—is the display of God's earnestness in seeking us, reconciling us to himself, making a fresh start possible.

Paul is also adamant about the quality of this reconciliation. People who have experienced estrangement in some relationship followed by reconciliation often find that the relationship is just not the same. New situations recall bad memories and feelings that then impose themselves in the present. In popular speech this is called "baggage." Paul uses such graphic language as "he forgave us all our misdeeds, wiping clean the record that stood against us with its legal demands, setting it aside by nailing it to the cross" (Col 2:13–14) to communicate to us that, as far as God is concerned, there is no baggage in our relationship with him based on what we were. The cross of Jesus is God's solemn declaration that he's not keeping a list in his head of all the things we have done wrong, as well as his earnest invitation to us to believe him. This gives us "boldness and access [to God] in confidence through [Christ's] faithfulness" (Eph 3:12).

Now the forgiveness of sins and restoration of relationship with God is all an important, indeed foundational, facet of "justification," one that Paul focuses on in several places. For example, Paul emphasizes this in Rom 4:1–12, most clearly in his quotation of Psa 32:1–2 as an explanation of "reckoning righteous": "Blessed are those whose transgressions are released, whose sins are covered over. Blessed is the person to whom

---

2. Daniel Bailey, *Jesus as the Mercy Seat: Paul's Use of Hilasterion in Romans 3:25* (Tübingen: Mohr Siebeck, forthcoming). This view is also given serious consideration by Charles Talbert in the course of his thorough consideration of the principal options (*Romans* [Macon, GA: Smyth & Helwys, 2002], 110–15).

God will not attribute sin."[3] In this initial justification we see the astounding generosity and kindness of God—that God should indeed forgive, and thus justify, the ungodly (Rom 4:5).[4] But a fresh start is just that—the *start* of the good news of our transformation.

YOU WERE FREED FROM BEING WHO YOU WERE TO BECOME HOLY AND JUST IN GOD'S SIGHT

Some people wander through life without ever engaging in real self-reflection. For such people, whatever's wrong in life is wrong because of some fault or failure of someone else. But if a person takes the time to look at who he or she has been, who he or she is now, it is probable that such a person would recognize that not everything about him- or herself is good, not everything is beautiful in God's sight. Indeed in our culture of blame, rights, and shifting responsibility to others, it is more and more of a triumph just to come to such self-knowledge. When we come to a true awareness of our self-centeredness, our failures in character and in action, Paul's gospel declares that we don't have to stay like this:

> For we ourselves were formerly senseless, disobedient, going astray, being enslaved to various desires and pleasures, living in malice and envy, hateful and hating one another. But when the goodness and beneficence of God, our Savior, manifested itself, *he delivered/saved us* (not on the grounds of works we performed in righteousness, but in accordance with his mercy) through the washing of a new creation ("regeneration") and through renewal effected by the Holy Spirit. This Spirit he poured out lavishly upon us through our Savior Jesus Christ in order that,

---

3. Mark Seifrid is thus correct to observe that, at this point at least, "the reckoning of righteousness is 'the non-reckoning of sin' (Rom 4:8; Ps 32:3)" ("Paul's Use of Righteousness Language against Its Hellenistic Background," in *Justification and Variegated Nomism*, ed. D. A. Carson, P. T. O'Brien, and Mark Seifrid, vol. 2, *The Paradoxes of Paul* [Mohr Siebeck: Tübingen, and Grand Rapids: Baker Academic, 2001] 61).

4. As Gottlob Schenk observes, this "*iustificatio iniusti* is against all human standards. The content bursts the forms and an act of grace replaces customary legal procedure" ("*Dikē*, etc.," in *Theological Dictionary of the New Testament*, ed. Gerhard Kittel, trans. G. W. Bromiley [Grand Rapids: Eerdmans, 1964], 2:205).

>after being made righteous [or "justified"] by Christ's
>gracious act, we might become heirs of eternal life in
>hope. This saying is reliable, and I want you to speak con-
>fidently concerning these things in order that those who
>have trusted in God may take care to focus on good works.
>(Titus 3:3–8)

In this text what people have been "saved from" is "what [they] formerly were"—"senseless, disobedient, going astray, being enslaved to various desires and pleasures, living in malice and envy, hateful and hating one another." They are saved to become something new, people with Spirit-directed practices. God has freed us specifically *not* to continue in those trajectories in which self-centeredness and sin—and even the sins of other people and the damage this has done to us—have impelled us.

I am reminded of something presented in many seventh- or eighth-grade science classes, namely the concept of inertia, which states that an object in motion tends to remain in motion at the same speed and in the same direction unless acted on by an imbalanced force. Our self-centered cravings and agendas kept us moving in a particular direction, but the cross of Jesus has the power to stop us in our tracks—as it did to Paul himself. Such a display of selflessness, of God-centeredness and other-centeredness, at the very least has to slow us down in our self-centered trajectory. And God's gift of the Holy Spirit introduces into our lives an imbalanced force, a force for which sin and self-centeredness are no equals, freeing us from the inertia, in effect, of the impulses of what Paul often calls our "former self," our "old self"—the "self" from which God saved us, because its end is the accumulation of a pile of injustices, harm to others, and condemnation for the failure to discover and live out God's purposes for the person God created. "All of us once lived among [those who are disobedient] in the passions of our flesh, following the desires of flesh and senses, and we were by nature children of wrath, like everyone else" (Eph 2:3 NRSV). We are freed to become "our best selves now"—which, if we were to think about this once again from Paul's point of view rather than from a self-centered, self-help perspective, doesn't mean our "selves" at all, but Christ coming alive in each one of us (as in Gal 2:19–20; 4:19). It is the recovery of the image of God within us through the incarnation of Jesus, who is indeed "the image of the eternal God" (Col 1:15), within us through the working of the Spirit.

The recovery of this image is the goal of our transformation. It is that toward which everything comes together—our trust in Jesus, God's filling us with the Holy Spirit, the Spirit's leading us into a new kind of life, even a new kind of being:

> If anyone is in Christ, new creation! The old things have passed away. Look! New things have come about! (2 Cor 5:17)

> Neither circumcision nor lack of circumcision means anything, but only a new creation. (Gal 6:15)

I would point out again that this transformation, this "new creation," matters very much to God. Indeed, the way Paul has put it in Galatians, it's the *only* thing that matters. Is Christ taking shape within us, coming to life within us, changing us from the inside out to be, to desire, and to do as Christ directs and as delights God?

You Were Freed to Live a Life of Doing Good

Some Protestant Christians are almost embarrassed about "good works," as if by doing them we might be seen to be seeking salvation by some means other than grace alone through faith. Paul, however, was certainly not embarrassed to speak about the importance of good works for those who call themselves Christians. In the first chapter we examined what kind of works Paul set in opposition to "faith" and found that these were not "good works," but rather the practices that set Jews apart from Gentiles on the assumption that the former were privileged in God's sight and the gatekeepers of God's kingdom.[5] As for "good works," Paul speaks of these as our whole reason for being. As "new creation," "we are God's handiwork, created in Christ Jesus for the purpose of good

---

5. On "works of the law," see David A. deSilva, *Global Readings: A Sri Lankan Commentary on Paul's Letter to the Galatians* (Eugene, OR: Wipf & Stock, 2011), 117-20, and the literature cited therein.

works which God prepared in advance, in order that we should walk in them" (Eph 2:10). This is expressed even more poignantly in one of the texts read every Christmas Eve for those who follow the Revised Common Lectionary:

> God's favor, bringing deliverance to all people, manifested itself [by] educating us to live justly and in a god-fearing manner during the present age, saying "No"[6] to ungodliness and worldly desires, while awaiting the blessed hope and manifestation of the glory of the great God and our savior Jesus Christ, who gave himself up on our behalf, in order that he might ransom us from every lawless deed and purify us to be a special people for himself that is fanatical for good works. (Titus 2:11–14)

What a purpose statement for God's acts on our behalf in Jesus! From this angle, God's grace includes an educative or training component, empowering us to "just say no" to the drives and impulses from within ourselves and from the world around us that push us in directions other than those in which the Spirit would lead us. Christ's purpose in giving himself for us was to make us a particular kind of people, a people *like him*, giving ourselves over to God to do the good works that God wishes to do in this world through us. According to this vision, we who call ourselves by Christ's name should be seen by others as *fanatics* for doing good,[7] acting generously, investing ourselves and our resources in others to relieve their need at whatever point that need exists.

At this point I want to circle back to Romans and explore how faith, transformation, and new kinds of action are held together—how transformation grows out of faith and rests fully on it, but also how faith means nothing and falls short of God's promise *without* transformation. This comes out clearly in the example of Abraham in Rom 4.

---

6. I have borrowed this apt idiomatic translation from the NIV 2011.

7. The Greek word here is *zēlōtēn*, denoting a particularly strong zeal or commitment to a cause or goal. It was the word chosen to describe the fanatical Judaean party that sought independence from Rome through armed revolution (hence the "Zealots").

Paul focuses on Abraham as a paradigm of justification, leaning heavily on the statement from Gen 15:6 that declares, "Abraham trusted God, and it was accounted to him for righteousness." Paul's major point in both places where he introduces Abraham as an example is that neither being circumcised (being inducted into the Jewish people and the Torah-driven life) nor *not* being circumcised has any bearing on meeting with God's approval (Rom 3:27-31; 4:9; Gal 3:6-9 in the context of the presenting issues of the letter, e.g., 5:2-4). Trusting God's promises is the path toward justification, toward being right with God.

A little-noticed facet of Abraham's example is that his trust in God's promise was *transformative*. Moreover, if it had not been transformative and if Abraham had not moved forward in the direction in which trust impelled him, the promise would never have been realized. The promise concerned descendants as numerous as the sand of the sea and the stars of the sky, but this all began to come about through an act of transformative obedience:

> Hoping against hope, he believed that he would become "the father of many nations," according to what was said, "So numerous shall your descendants be." He did not weaken in faith when he considered his own body, which was already as good as dead (for he was about a hundred years old), or when he considered the barrenness of Sarah's womb. No distrust made him waver concerning the promise of God, but he grew strong in his faith as he gave glory to God, being fully convinced that God was able to do what he had promised. *Therefore* his faith "was reckoned to him as righteousness." (Rom 4:18-22 NRSV, emphasis mine)

Abraham's trust led him to act in line with the promise, to have sex with Sarah in the expectation of her becoming pregnant, trusting that God would make this act effective (i.e., that they would become people capable of having a son) in spite of all the available arguments to the contrary. In Paul's fuller accounting of Abraham's faith it is not just his belief but his acting in line with that belief that leads to his faith being accounted to him as righteousness. Without such trust-inspired action the promise would have failed.[8] Falling in line with the example of Abraham entails not just bare trust, but trusting obedience—the obedience that comes from faith (Rom 1:6; 16:26)—that leads us forward toward God's promised goal.

Paul often defines the new life negatively in terms of how it no longer includes practices and attitudes that characterized the "old" life. But texts like those we have explored here with their emphasis on the constructive doing of what is good remind us that being brought into alignment with God's standards is not just about abstaining from what is wicked. It is also about the positive investment of ourselves in the good, in the life of the new person, in allowing Christ to do in this world as Christ wishes through us, who are now elements of the body that must be fully responsive to the commands and desires of the head. The view from the negative side is this: "Don't you know that your bodies are parts of Christ's body? Should I therefore take parts of Christ's body and join them to a whore?" (1 Cor 6:15). From this side it's a question of thinking about what *I* will do or not do with *my* body out of consideration for what it means for Christ's body. The view from the positive side is this: "It's not *me* living anymore, but Christ living in me" (Gal 2:19). From this side it's a question of Christ thinking about what to do with this part of his body that is me (or, at another level, with this part of his body that is the congregation to which I belong), and my discerning this in the Spirit and yielding to it.

Transformation Means a Putting Off and a Putting On

Paul uses several metaphors to help us think about the task and process of transformation. He uses the language of a former self and a new person. He uses the language of laying something aside like a dirty set of clothing and putting on something fresh like a set of clean clothing.

---

8. In Seifrid's examination of this "later stage in Abraham's story," he does not give any attention to Abraham having to act in line with his trust in order for God's purposes and promise to come to fruition. He notes instead that "Paul pictures Abraham not merely as actor, but more fundamentally as one acted upon by the promise of God: 'he was made strong in faith' (Rom 4:20)" ("Paul's Use," 62). But strong for what? Seifrid does not say.

He speaks most radically about dying to something old and rising to something new.

> Now this I affirm and insist on in the Lord: you must no longer live as the Gentiles live, in the futility of their minds. They are darkened in their understanding, alienated from the life of God because of their ignorance and hardness of heart. ... You were taught to put away your former way of life, your old self, corrupt and deluded by its lusts, and to be renewed in the spirit of your minds, and to clothe yourselves with the new self, created according to the likeness of God in true righteousness and holiness. (Eph 4:17–18, 22–24 NRSV)

In texts like these Paul expands on what it means to be a "new creation" and how this new creation takes shape out of the chaos of our old selves, over which God's Spirit is brooding afresh.

This process of change is one that depends both on God's active investment and on ours as we continue to respond to the favor and the help he has given us. It requires ongoing attention, discernment, and commitment to continue to lay aside what is not from the Spirit and to take up what is. Paul himself was quite aware of how strenuous this process was in his own life and how constant he needed to be in attending to making progress:

> Don't you know that, while all runners compete in a race, only one receives the prize? Run in such a manner that you may attain it. Everyone engaged in an athletic competition exercises self-control in regard to everything. These people do so in order that they might receive a wreath that will wither, but we do it to gain a wreath that will never wither. So I don't run without purpose, neither do I box as one who beats the air; but I pummel my body and subdue it, so that after proclaiming the good news to others I should not be disqualified myself. (1 Cor 9:24–27)

We are generally aware of the commitment, endurance, and self-discipline that programs of physical exercise involve and how easy it is to slack off or give up altogether. Paul tells us that we need to be prepared to give the same kind of commitment and investment of ourselves to God's program of "training us to live justly and in a god-fearing manner during the present age, saying 'No' to ungodliness and worldly desires" (to borrow again from Titus), and to persevere in this to the end, since we're not doing it merely to lose weight or fend off heart disease but to make the full and appropriate use of God's gifts that lead to our salvation. I can't fail to notice, in light of the ease with which so many speak of "eternal security," how in this text even Paul acknowledges the danger to his own soul of failing to engage the contest God has set before him—"so that after proclaiming the good news to others I should not be disqualified myself."[9]

In his letter to the Christians in Colossae, Paul paints a helpful portrait of the life of the "old person" and the life of the "new self"—one that provides an ever-helpful diagnostic tool, as it were, for the task of self-examination:

> Put to death, then, those parts of you that belong to the world: fornication, impurity, passion, selfish desire, and greed, which is idolatry. God's wrath is coming upon the disobedient on account of these things. You also used to walk in these things, when you were living that life. But now put them all aside—anger, wrath, malice, slander, and abusive language from your mouth. Don't keep lying to one another, since you stripped off the old self

---

9. Schenk ("*Dikē*, etc.," 208) elucidates the tension between Paul's assurance of deliverance and his wholehearted investment of himself in the work of transformation thus: "Paul did not regard the final judgment by works as contradicting justification by faith. ... The new assurance is characterized as a tireless pursuit of the goal, and kept from false confidence, by the seriousness of judgment. This does not mean that assurance of salvation is either shaken or called in question. The point is that the thought of judgment serves as a powerful motive to obedience. The doctrine of justification demands encounter with the unsparing seriousness of God expressed at the cross." The final statement is particularly important as it touches on the attitude of the disciple: The seriousness of the crucifixion of Jesus calls forth our own seriousness about dying with and living for Jesus, giving ourselves over to the work of God initiated at the cross—and at such cost.

with its practices and clothed yourselves with the new self, which is being renewed in knowledge according to the image of the One who created it. In this renewal there isn't Greek and Jew, circumcised and uncircumcised, barbarian, Scythian, slave, free person. Rather, Christ is all things and in all!

Clothe yourselves, then, as God's chosen, holy, and loved ones, *with deeply felt compassion, kindness, humility, forbearance, and patience.* Bear with one another and be gracious toward one another, if anyone has a complaint against another. In the same way as the Lord was gracious to you, so be gracious yourselves as well. On top of everything else, *clothe yourselves with love,* which holds it all together perfectly. And let the peace of Christ rule in your hearts, to which indeed you were called in the one body. And be thankful. Let the word of Christ dwell in you richly; teach and admonish one another in all wisdom; and with gratitude in your hearts sing psalms, hymns, and spiritual songs to God. And whatever you do, in word or deed, do everything in the name of the Lord Jesus, giving thanks to God the Father through him. (Col 3:5–17)

This text provides a fairly detailed picture—with some good, nitty-gritty examples—of what it means to die with Christ and to "put on Christ," or to walk in newness of life (Rom 6:4). Along with similar passages among Paul's writings, it also suggests a particular and different sort of agenda for Christ's followers day by day—every day. It is an agenda that ought to lie beneath every other agenda and that every other agenda should serve to advance within us. This agenda has to do with taking off, laying aside, and dying to some familiar ways, and with putting on, draping over ourselves, and coming alive in new ways.

Several spiritual disciplines are necessary to accomplish this. I would especially highlight Scripture reading, prayer, self-examination, and holy conferencing. As we immerse ourselves in Scripture, we encounter images of the many symptoms that help us diagnose when our old self, the self from which Jesus died to deliver us, is asserting itself. We read of the internal and relational qualities and the practical fruit that show us what it looks like when the Spirit is leading us, when Christ is taking fuller shape within us. As we pray and examine ourselves before God, practicing openness, vulnerability, and silence before God, his Spirit brings the Word to bear on us as we are in that moment, sometimes convicting, sometimes affirming. As we band together with other Christians similarly committed to transformation, we share insights into one another and help one another see the blind spots, see from outside our own perspective on ourselves.

All of these practices are essential. We need to ask ourselves regularly: Is what I am about to do, or the way I am relating to someone, or this particular practice in which I am engaging the result of my offering my mind, heart, and body to God? Or is something that I have been doing, am doing, or am thinking about doing the result of my offering myself to do my own bidding—the bidding of self-centered, self gratifying impulses? We can't fool God's Spirit within us with our answers; if we immerse ourselves enough in Scripture, in prayer, and in conversation with people who are seeking to live for God, we can't fool ourselves with our answers for too long, either. And, as soon as we know the answer to these questions, we know what we need to do. This is where commitment and self-denial come into play. To return to Paul's analogy: the athlete has to say "no" to a lot that he or she would prefer to enjoy or to do if he or she is to become better in the area in which he or she would compete. So we also have to die to a lot that is almost hardwired within us, to responses and impulses that are as automatic as instinct, if we are to arrive at the life God desires for us.

John Wesley seemed to intuit this. When he penned his "Prayers for Daily Use" for serious Christians to use specifically to make progress in this transformation, he gave the focal virtue of "mortification," of dying to our own cravings, desires, agendas, and self-absorption, two days out of the week.[10] It is a dying, and dying is never pleasant. But what prom-

---

10. Wesley's seven-day cycle of self-examination and prayer each morning and evening focuses on nurturing what he identified as the cardinal Christian virtues of love for God, love for neighbor, humility, mortification, resignation, and gratitude. For an updated paraphrase in a more modern devotional format, see David A. deSilva, *Praying with John Wesley* (Nashville: Discipleship Resources, 2001).

ises to come to life in place of what we put to death within us is noble and beautiful, of such a quality as unites us further with God and bears the most eloquent witness to the truth of the gospel and its power.

God Makes This Transformation Possible through the Gift of the Holy Spirit

If the work of this transformation sat squarely within the realm of our effort and obligation, it would not be "good news" at all. Paul, however, proclaimed a God who was both righteous himself *and* able to make the person who trusts Jesus righteous as well (Rom 3:26). An essential part of his "good news" is that God desires and requires nothing that God does not himself also nurture and empower. God has sent his Spirit into our hearts and into our midst to guide and direct us as individuals and as communities of faith, not merely to empower our *struggle* against sin and self-centered desire but to enable our *victory* over the same.[11]

A close study of Galatians reveals how important and how central the Holy Spirit is to Paul's conception of God's new work among us in Jesus. A great deal of the argument in Paul's response to the Galatians, and presumably therefore among the parties arguing in Galatia at the time, had to do with how one became an heir of Abraham and thereby an heir of God's promises and a part of God's people. In Paul's understanding:

> Christ redeemed us [Jewish believers] from the curse of
> the Torah by becoming a curse on our behalf, as it is writ-
> ten, "Cursed is everyone who hangs on a tree," in order

---

11. N. T. Wright correctly discerns the role of the Spirit in bringing us to our final state of being people in whom God sees righteousness reflected: "You cannot ... have a Pauline doctrine of assurance (and the glory of the Reformation doctrine of justification is precisely assurance) without the Pauline doctrine of the Spirit" (*Justification: God's Plan and Paul's Vision* [Downers Grove, IL: InterVarsity Press, 2009], 237). I would affirm the necessity of the working of the third person of the Trinity if, indeed, "the final outcome is never put in doubt" for those who trust in Jesus (Michael Bird, *The Saving Righteousness of God: Studies on Paul, Justification and the New Perspective* [Milton Keynes, UK: Paternoster, 2007], 175), not to suggest that Jesus' obedience unto death is insufficient for our final justification (Bird's pressing concern), but rather to suggest that we depend on the Spirit to bring to life that obedience within us. The "we" who cannot be separated from God's love (Rom 8:38–39) are "those in whom the Spirit is working his life-giving, free-Christian-holiness-producing revolution (Romans 8:5–8; 12:1–2)" (Wright, *Justification*, 238).

> that Abraham's blessing might come upon the nations in
> Christ Jesus—in order that we might receive the promised
> Spirit by trusting. (Gal 3:13-14, citing Deut 27:26)

The promise given to Abraham—a promise that the giving of the Torah could not alter or amend—is, for Paul, nothing other than the Holy Spirit whose presence, activity, and indwelling was a fundamental facet of the early church's experience.[12] The giving of the Holy Spirit is a climactic point in God's dealings with humanity, nothing less than the fulfillment of the promise that, in Abraham, all the nations would receive blessing. It is this Holy Spirit, moreover, that is the God-given means of working in us the righteousness that the Torah could not (Gal 2:21; 3:21; 5:5).

Trusting in Jesus for our justification includes, for Paul, trusting that what Jesus has secured for us through his death, namely the gift of the indwelling Holy Spirit, is sufficient to lead us through, and bring about within us, this transformation that brings us in line with God's righteous standards. In other words, "being justified by means of trust" involves "being aligned with God's standards of righteousness by the means that God provides to those who trust," namely the Spirit.

> But I say, keep walking by the Spirit and you will certain-
> ly not fulfill what the flesh desires. For the flesh yearns
> against the Spirit's leanings, and the Spirit against the
> flesh's leanings, for these stand opposed to one anoth-
> er in order that you may not do whatever you want. ...
> And those who are Christ's crucified the flesh along with
> its passions and desires. If we live by the Spirit, let's also
> keep falling in step with the Spirit. (Gal 5:16-17, 24-25)

Paul's converts in Galatia are very much aware of the importance of living in line with God's righteousness and of finding the necessary

---

12. Wright (*Justification*, 124) takes the two clauses in Gal 3:14 in two separate senses, with the "we" indicating "presumably Jews who believe in Jesus" as recipients of the promised Spirit (see also 125, 171). Paul uses "we" elsewhere in Galatians to refer specifically to Jewish Christians, as in Gal 2:15-16, where Paul articulates the common ground between himself, Peter, and the people from James. Restricting the "we" in Gal 3:14 to Jewish Christians, however, would be problematic in light of the emphasis Paul places on the Galatians—as *Gentiles*—receiving this same Spirit in 3:2-5; 4:6-7.

means to resist the impulses of their own self-centered interests and urges. This is what attracted them to the message of Paul's rivals, who presented the Torah-regulated life as God's answer to those problems. Paul promises, on the contrary, that God's Spirit is not only a sufficient but a superior resource: "[K]eep on walking as the Spirit directs, and you will surely not fulfill the flesh's impulses."[13]

The promise of Gal 5:16 controls how we should read 5:17: "the flesh yearns against the Spirit's leanings, and the Spirit against the flesh's leanings, for these stand opposed to one another in order that you may not do whatever you want." This verse is not describing a state of paralysis, as if the Spirit and the flesh are equal powers and we are caught in a perpetual stalemate.[14] Rather the Spirit is the stronger power; allying ourselves with the Spirit assures the defeat of our self-centered impulses.[15]

I point this out because many Christians do not believe that they have been set free from the power of sin and self-centered desire. They mistake their ongoing experience of struggle and their occasional failures for the status quo of life in the body. This is *not* good news, and it is certainly not *Paul's* good news. Theologians have helped reinforce this conviction with—and here I am fairly confident—a *mis*reading of a key Pauline text: Rom 7:7-25.

There are two principal approaches to this passage. One of them reads it as a description of the condition of the Christian:[16] "I can desire what is noble, but cannot do it; for I don't do the good thing that I want

---

13. The NRSV mistranslates the second verb as another command rather than as an assured consequence: "Live by the Spirit, I say, and do not gratify the desires of the flesh" (Gal 5:16). Paul uses, however, a construction that expresses an emphatic negation of future consequences, hence, "and you will certainly not gratify the flesh's desires."

14. Against H. D. Betz, *Galatians*, Hermeneia (Philadelphia: Fortress, 1979), 279–80; Richard Longenecker, *Galatians*, WBC (Dallas: Word, 1990), 246.

15. As Bird (*Saving Righteousness*, 173) observes, "Paul's anthropological pessimism about the human inability to keep the law is matched only by his pneumatological optimism that Spirit-empowered persons will be able to fulfill the requirements of the law when they walk in the Spirit (Rom. 8.4; Gal. 5.25) and fulfill the law of Moses and Christ (Rom. 13.8–10; Gal. 6.2)." See also Troels Engberg-Pedersen, *Paul and the Stoics* (Louisville: Westminster John Knox, 2000), 163, 165; J. M. G. Barclay, *Obeying the Truth: Paul's Ethics in Galatians* (Minneapolis: Fortress, 1991), 115–16.

16. See, for example, Don Garlington, *Faith, Obedience, and Perseverance* (Tübingen: Mohr Siebeck, 1994), ch. 5.

to do, but the bad thing I don't want to do, *this* I do" (7:18-19). While we may resonate with the struggle that Paul describes, it is important for us to realize that he himself is *not* describing what he believes to be the standard condition of the person who is in Christ. It is consequently a mistake for us to throw up our hands in the face of our own struggles against sinful and self-centered impulses, quote this verse or some other part of this passage, give up, and give in. This section is instead essentially a vindication of the Torah, answering the question "What then shall we say? That the Torah is sin? Heck, no!" (Rom 7:7). God's law is good, but sin has so pervaded humanity that the Torah lacks the power to bring people into alignment with God's righteousness. The passage is an explanation of how the Torah's failure is not a fault inherent in the Torah.[17]

When Paul says in this context, "I am of the flesh, having been sold *under sin*" (7:14b), he describes once again the state of the person, in this case particularly the Jew, prior to God's gracious intervention in his or her life bringing that person to trust in Jesus and to receive the gift of the Holy Spirit. It is comparable to the claim he makes earlier in Rom 3:9: "We have already concluded that Jews and Gentiles are *under sin.*" This state of being "under sin," controlled by sin, under sin's power and jurisdiction, even "slaves" to sin, is the state from which people are delivered in Jesus. *That* is the good news.[18] Paul had in fact made this abundantly clear in the preceding chapter:

> Our old self was crucified with him in order that the body characterized by sin might be made powerless, in order that we might no longer live as slaves to sin. ... Sin shall not dominate you. ... Thanks be to God that you *were* slaves of sin but you *have become* obedient from the heart. ... *Freed from sin*, you were enslaved to righteousness. (Rom 6:6, 14, 17-18)

17. See James D. G. Dunn, *The Theology of Paul the Apostle* (Grand Rapids: Eerdmans, 1998), 157.
18. On the reading of Rom 7:7-25 as a description of the unregenerate person rather than the believer who is in Christ, see also Talbert, *Romans*, 188-89.

Paul has taken a step to the side in his argument in 7:7-25, talking about the person "under Torah" and his or her experience of being dominated by sin because of the power of the flesh, "this body of death" as he puts it in Rom 7:24. Such a person experiences a terrible rift within his or her own being: "So then, I myself am a slave to God's law in my mind, but to sin's law in my flesh." The divided self that Paul describes in 7:25 is not the state in which Christ has left the one who trusts him. Rather, it is the state from which God has set the believer free in Christ, as Paul goes on to say: "The law of the Spirit of life *has set you free* in Christ from the law of sin and death" (8:2). This is the reason for Paul's somewhat premature declaration of praise a few verses before: "Thanks be to God through our Lord Jesus Christ!" in response to his agonized question, "Who will rescue me from this body of death?" (7:24). God has taken in hand to free us from the power of sin and allow us to enter a new kind of life in the power of the Spirit, a life in which we, obedient from the heart, fulfill the righteous standard that God had sought to cultivate through the Torah:

> God has done what the law, weakened by the flesh, could not do: by sending his own Son in the likeness of sinful flesh, and to deal with sin, he condemned sin in the flesh, *so that the just requirement of the law might be fulfilled in us,* who walk not according to the flesh but according to the Spirit. (Rom 8:3-4 NRSV)

Paul doesn't speak anywhere of Christians *doing* the law, but he does speak of Christians *fulfilling* the law (see also Gal 5:13-14; Rom 13:8-10), accomplishing by another means what the law was after all along—and that means is the Holy Spirit, given as a guide and even as a champion to overcome the drives and impulses of the flesh.[19]

This requires from us once again that we set our minds—our intent, our commitment, our focus—steadfastly and consistently on the Spirit and its leading rather than on the flesh (in effect, that self-centered and self-gratifying instinct within us) and its leading.

---

19. See Betz, *Galatians*, 275; Barclay, *Obeying the Truth*, 138.

> For those who live according to the flesh set their minds
> on the things of the flesh, but those who live according
> to the Spirit set their minds on the things of the Spirit.
> To set the mind on the flesh is death, but to set the mind
> on the Spirit is life and peace. For this reason the mind
> that is set on the flesh is hostile to God; it does not sub-
> mit to God's law—indeed it cannot, and those who are in
> the flesh cannot please God. But you are not in the flesh;
> you are in the Spirit, since the Spirit of God dwells in you.
> (Rom 8:5–9a NRSV)

These selections from Rom 8 take us back to a point that has impressed itself on me more and more as I study Paul: God will finally acquit us because he has enabled us to become and to do what is good and just in his sight.

You Are Free from the Fear of Death

No account of Paul's good news would be complete without giving notice to the final stage in this process of transformation, the transformation of our death-bound bodies that marks our entrance into life beyond death:

> Our citizenship is in heaven, and it is from there that
> we are expecting a Savior, the Lord Jesus Christ. He will
> transform the body of our humiliation that it may be
> conformed to the body of his glory, by the power that
> also enables him to make all things subject to himself.
> (Phil 3:20–21 NRSV)

> When this perishable body puts on imperishability, and
> this mortal body puts on immortality, then the saying that
> is written will be fulfilled: "Death has been swallowed up
> in victory." … Therefore, my beloved, be steadfast, im-
> movable, always excelling in the work of the Lord, be-
> cause you know that in the Lord your labor is not in vain.
> (1 Cor 15:54, 58 NRSV)

The good news is not just that the one who trusts in Jesus is free to become a new person in Christ; it is also that this new person he or she is becoming will live forever. When Paul declares that "the last enemy to be destroyed is death" (1 Cor 15:26 NRSV), he speaks about the defeat of the universal enemy of the human race. His "good news" is that the one who trusts Christ need live no longer under the shadow of the fear of death, since God has made provision for death no longer to be the final word on human existence.

Believing this is the key to committed discipleship. Thinking that this life is all we have is in many ways the power source for our self-centered impulses and desires. If we look at death as a dead end and at this life as the primary arena for our fulfillment, then self-gratification becomes more important and self-denial for the sake of seeking the good of others or the advancement of God's agenda becomes less reasonable. The author of the Wisdom of Solomon, an earlier contemporary of Paul, expressed this mindset eloquently:

> Our lives are short and painful. There is no antidote for death; no one has come back from the grave. All of us came into being by chance. When our lives are over, it will be just as if we had never been. ... Come then! Let's enjoy all the good things of life now. Let's enjoy creation to the fullest as we did in our youth. Let's drink our fill of expensive wines and enjoy fine perfumes. Let's pluck every fresh blossom of spring as we pass by. Let's crown ourselves with rosebuds before they wither. Let's make sure that no meadow is left untouched by our high-spirited fun. Let's leave evidence everywhere that we made the most of this life, because this life is all we have. Let's take advantage of the day laborer who does what's right. Let's not be afraid to abuse the widow. Let's show that we couldn't care less for the gray hair of our elders. May strength be our only law and determine what's right, for it's clear to us that what is weak is worthless. (Wis 2:1-2, 6-11 CEB)

The author suggests that, when self-gratification during life is a high priority, it is an easy step to move from being simply neglectful of the well-being of others to embracing predatory practices to satisfy one's own desires at the expense of one's weaker neighbors.

Wisdom of Solomon describes this mindset as the result of making a "covenant with death" (1:16), of agreeing, in effect, with death's ultimate claim on one's life and living accordingly within the confines of an interest in this life only. The book also indicts this mindset as the result of a failure to grasp God's ultimate purposes for human beings:

> They didn't hope for the reward that holiness brings. They didn't consider the prize they would win if they kept their souls free from stain. God created humans to live forever. He made them as a perfect representation of his own unique identity. (Wis 2:22–23 CEB)

Hope for this final transformation empowers investment in the whole process up to that last stage.

Paul understands this very well. Indeed he himself admits that, if he is wrong about God's promise of life beyond death, he, his team, and his converts are "of all people most to be pitied" (1 Cor 15:19 NRSV), since they will have neglected the pleasures and comforts of this life in favor of a life that is *not* to come.

> If the dead are not raised at all, … why are we putting ourselves in danger every hour? If with merely human hopes I fought with wild animals at Ephesus, what would I have gained by it? If the dead are not raised, "Let us eat and drink, for tomorrow we die." (1 Cor 15:29–30, 32 NRSV)

While one who does not believe in a life beyond death need not sacrifice some sense of pursuing nobility for its own sake, as many have proven in the course of history, not having such a belief puts serious limits on what one might sacrifice or the hardships one might embrace for this pursuit. Because of his hope for the final transformation, however, Paul is able to invest all that he is in this present life into the cause of God without the fear that his *temporal* losses are *actual* losses.

> We do not lose heart. Even though our outer nature is
> wasting away, our inner nature is being renewed day by
> day. For this slight momentary affliction is preparing us
> for an eternal weight of glory beyond all measure, be-
> cause we look not at what can be seen but at what cannot
> be seen; for what can be seen is temporary, but what can-
> not be seen is eternal. (2 Cor 4:16–18 NRSV)

Paul's radical obedience to God's commission to proclaim the "good news" throughout the Roman Mediterranean is rooted in this mind-set. So is his commitment to see God's transformation of his own life from that of a respected devotee of the strictest path within Judaism into that of one who bears in his own body the marks and experience of the mar-ginalized and crucified Messiah (Gal 6:17).

The more we live for the enjoyment of the pleasures, prestige, and property of this life, the less we will invest of ourselves in the pro-cess of transformation that leads to the enjoyment of what is eternal. In the words attributed to Jesus, "those who seek to make their lives secure will lose them; those who lose their lives for my sake and the sake of the Gospel will make them secure" (Mark 8:35). If we believe Paul's words about the end of this process of transformation—sharing in the resur-rected life of the one with whom we died to ourselves—we will not hold ourselves back from pursuing that process fully during this life.

CHAPTER 3

The Gospel Means the Transformation of Community: You Are Free to Relate to One Another in New Ways

The preceding chapters have been dedicated to exploring a new overarching metaphor for the rescue that God has provided for us in Jesus from our situation of estrangement from God, our state of having been subdued by sin and knocked way out of alignment with God, orbiting instead around ourselves and our self-protective and self-gratifying impulses. In answer to the question of how God can both himself remain "just" while also declaring us to be "just" when we stand before his judgment seat, I've suggested that the answer lies in the metaphor of transformation, and indeed that this metaphor lies at the heart of Paul's "good news." God has set aside humanity's offenses against himself, sending his Son as a demonstration of God's love and commitment to reconciliation with all the people groups of the world, first the Jew and also the non-Jew, and pouring his Spirit into us to free us from the power of sin and self-centered desire to live in a manner that is truly righteous before God.

But we must look further into Paul, particularly in our culture of individualism and in the religious climate of "personal decision" that has dominated a good deal of (especially) Protestant thought and practice. God's intervention is not just about the transformation of individuals. It is also about the formation of a people for himself—what Paul in his more poetic moments will speak of collectively as Christ's bride (2 Cor 11:2). Paul expresses a vision in which God is not only transforming individuals but is transforming individuals-in-community, people who are part of one another, parts of a much greater whole that is collectively the focus of God's saving action.

The Transformation of Strangers into Family, Many Bodies into One Body

The two principal images that Paul uses to speak about the *ekklēsia*, the people called out to gather as God's assembly, are "family" and "body." He dedicates a fair amount of space in his writing to the task of changing the way his readers think about one another, replacing many other labels and categories with these two. This is because he understands that people who are "in Christ" need to act toward one another and respond to one another in ways that would be unnatural if they continued to see one another according to their relationships in the world: strangers or passing acquaintances, competitors, outsiders, foreigners, people of other races, and the like. Conversely, people who are together "in Christ" *cannot* continue to act and respond toward one another in ways that would align naturally with these former categories of relationship.

Paul casts a vision, therefore, for how God has transformed our relationships. God has adopted us all into his own family, making us all children of one parent and sisters and brothers to the many others God has brought into his family:

> In Christ Jesus you are all children of God through faith. (Gal 3:26 NRSV)

> When the fullness of time had come, God sent his Son, born of a woman, born under the law, in order to redeem those who were under the law, so that we might receive adoption as children. And because you are children, God

> has sent the Spirit of his Son into our hearts, crying,
> "Abba! Father!" (Gal 4:4-6 NRSV)

Because the good news included becoming adopted children of God, "brother" and "sister" became the most common way for Christian leaders like Paul to address their converts, reminding them at every turn of their transformed social reality.[1] Whatever they once were to each other on the basis of the settings and structures of the world, they were now kin to one another to an intimate degree. Their relationships with—and investments in—one another were to reflect this new relational reality, and thus they would indeed become a transformed community: the household of God. As family, it would be natural and expected for them to invest themselves in meeting one another's needs, forgiving, working toward reconciliation and restoration, treating one another with the honor and esteem of fellow children of God—and all this toward people who might well have been strangers prior to their conversion, or members of estranged ethnic groups, or people separated by economic chasms.[2]

But even the image of "one family" wasn't sufficient for the task of articulating the transformation God was nurturing among those who shared trust in the Son and who received a share in God's Spirit. On several occasions Paul reaches for an even more radical image of intimate interconnection: believers have become parts of a single organism, the body of which Christ is the head.

> We, who are many, are one body in Christ, and individually we are members one of another. (Rom 12:5 NRSV)

---

1. It is unfortunate that, in the laudable attempt to achieve gender inclusivity where appropriate, some translations replace the kinship term adelphoi with terms that do not invoke the bonds and ethos of the sibling relationship, even though early Christian authors were intentionally evoking and nurturing that ethos. The NRSV, for example, often renders adelphoi as "friends" (Rom 7:4; 1 Cor 14:26, 36; 2 Cor 11:9; Gal 4:12, 28, 31; 5:11; 6:1; Phil 4:21) or "beloved" (1 Cor 15:58; Phil 1:12; 3:13; 4:8; 1 Thess 4:10; 5:4, 14, 25; 2 Thess 3:6) rather than simply (and accurately) "brothers and sisters."

2. Further on the ethos of siblings in the ancient world and the ways in which Paul and other early Christian authors invoke this ethos among Christians, see David A. deSilva, *Honor, Patronage, Kinship & Purity: Unlocking New Testament Culture* (Downers Grove, IL: InterVarsity Press, 2000), 165-73, 212-25.

> For just as the body is one and has many members, and
> all the members of the body, though many, are one body,
> so it is with Christ. For in the one Spirit we were all bap-
> tized into one body—Jews or Greeks, slaves or free—and
> we were all made to drink of one Spirit. Indeed, the body
> does not consist of one member but of many. ... Now you
> are the body of Christ and individually members of it.
> (1 Cor 12:12–14, 27 NRSV)

The image of many human beings together forming a single organism,
a single body, was familiar to Paul from Stoic philosophers, who sought
to nurture two things through this image: an appreciation of the differentiation between particular individuals, each being constituted
and skilled in such a way as contributes to the well-being of the entire
society, and an ethos of cooperation rather than competition among
people. Competition has marked—and marred—human interaction at
the level of individuals and at the level of groups for a long time indeed.
The image of a social group (indeed all of creation) as a single body was
intended to help people move beyond seeing one another as a threat to
their own thriving and their own enjoyment of limited goods to seeing
one another as co-contributors to one another's thriving—and indeed
being deeply committed to one another's thriving rather than fundamentally only to one's own.[3]

Paul takes up both facets of the Stoics' social ethics, calling people to
recognize and honor their own and one another's contributions to the
spectrum of the church's functioning, to see one another as highly differ-
entiated parts of a well-functioning body. Paul brings this out wherever
he uses the body metaphor for the local and global Christian community:

> The gifts [Christ] gave were that some would be apostles,
> some prophets, some evangelists, some pastors and teach-
> ers, *to equip the saints* for the work of ministry, *for building*

---

3. A. A. Long, *Epictetus: A Stoic and Socratic Guide to Life* (Oxford: Oxford University Press, 2002),
21. The image was also applied to the body politic of the city, often to urge cooperation and
harmony for the common good, without which there would be no individual good (see David
Garland, *1 Corinthians*, BECNT [Grand Rapids: Baker Academic, 2003]), 592–94.

up the body of Christ, until all of us come to the unity of the faith and of the knowledge of the Son of God, to maturity, to the measure of the full stature of Christ. ... We must grow up in every way into him who is the head, into Christ, from whom the whole body, joined and knit together by every ligament with which it is equipped, as each part is working properly, promotes the body's growth in building itself up in love. (Eph 4:11-13, 15-16 NRSV, emphasis added)

To each is given the manifestation of the Spirit for the common good. To one is given through the Spirit the utterance of wisdom, and to another the utterance of knowledge according to the same Spirit, to another faith by the same Spirit, to another gifts of healing by the one Spirit, to another the working of miracles, to another prophecy, to another the discernment of spirits, to another various kinds of tongues, to another the interpretation of tongues. All these are activated by one and the same Spirit, who allots to each one individually just as the Spirit chooses. For just as the body is one and has many members, and all the members of the body, though many, are one body, so it is with Christ. (1 Cor 12:7-12 NRSV)

We, who are many, are one body in Christ, and individually we are members one of another. We have gifts that differ according to the grace given to us: prophecy, in proportion to faith; ministry, in ministering; the teacher, in teaching; the exhorter, in exhortation; the giver, in generosity; the leader, in diligence; the compassionate, in cheerfulness. (Rom 12:5-8 NRSV)

The point of the image, at least in part, is that we are dependent on one another for our own transformation. We are, individually and collectively, part of God's mechanism for fostering this process of transformation in one another. We need what each other has to offer if we are to persevere and remain consistent in our own journeys of transformation. Therefore each one of us needs to offer to the others in the body whatever we have, whatever God gives us, at every opportunity, so that they will persevere and remain consistent in their journeys of transformation.

When each part is working properly—when each of us is both becoming what God is nurturing within us and offering what God gives us for the nurturing of others in their becoming—the result is that we all come closer to the goal and end of our transformation. Where individual disciples are not growing and where congregations are experiencing atrophy, it is likely that we are failing to invest in one another. Once more this pushes us past the level of polite social interaction with one another to a level of intimate investment in one another's lives, progress in the faith, and points of need.

Paul's use of the image of a single body for a group of human beings differs from popular Stoic uses in at least one very important respect. The Stoics spoke of a divine spirit that animated the whole, but Paul identifies a specific person as the "head" of this "body," namely Christ. This is the social counterpart of Paul's declaration concerning his own experience of living in the Spirit: "It's no longer *me* living, but *Christ* is living in me" (Gal 2:19). In Paul's vision for the Church, Christ, to the extent that he animates each person, animates and directs the whole body as well. Body parts cannot just pursue their own interests or move at their own impulses. When that happens we witness ungraceful spasms and convulsions. But when the body moves at the initiative and direction of a single mind, its parts are united into graceful motions and purposeful actions.

Paul's Guidance for Living as a Transformed and Transforming Community

Paul is often celebrated as a great missionary figure, taking the gospel from place to place, preaching, forming congregations, and moving on. He indeed deserves to be thus celebrated, but we should not neglect Paul's work as a *pastor* of the churches he founded. Indeed most of his surviving correspondence represents pastoral interventions in the communities he left behind, as he continued to give them guidance and direction, seeking to keep them headed toward what he believed to be God's vision for their interactions, involvements, and witness. As a result, he has left a great deal of material from which to reconstruct this vision, providing a basis for reflection on the transformation he would continue to wish to see nurtured in contemporary faith communities.

Restorative Intervention

Paul understands that each person on this journey of transformation needs the support, guidance, and even correction of others in the household of God. When someone in the congregation starts going down a path that takes him or her away from the transformation God's Spirit would work within each person, his or her fellow believers could choose any one of a number of unhelpful responses. They could ignore it on the pretext of not wishing to be meddlesome. They could talk to one another about it and agree together how terrible, sad, or shameful it is, and wonder how the congregation can tolerate such a thing. They could subtly start making the person feel uncomfortable in the Christian community. None of these responses helps the individual get back on track. Paul thus advises:

> Brothers and sisters, if any person is overtaken by some transgression, restore such a person, you in whom the Spirit dwells, in a spirit of forbearance, watching yourself lest you also be tested. Keep bearing one another's burdens, and in this way you will fulfill Christ's law. (Gal 6:1–2)

He urges people within this transformed and transforming community known as the church to do what would be natural to do for someone in one's own family, who grew up in the same house. One would go to the person, clothed in humility, gentleness, and compassion, and talk to him or her about what one saw happening because one cared deeply about that person and what happens to him or her. One would ask such a person to examine whether it's really in line with his or her own best desires for him- or herself in the Lord or with what God wishes to do in his or her life.

Such a response would provide the straying sister or brother with a chance to start talking about what's behind the behavior and would also open up an opportunity for God to begin the process of healing whatever it is, robbing it of its power over the person. And the sister or brother would know that he or she isn't facing that situation alone. Paul wisely counsels the other members of the household of faith to remember that they are also not immune from any sin or misstep that their sister or brother has made, which should result in the appropriate "forbearance" or "meekness" (Gal 6:1) in dealing with an erring sister or brother.[4] Such interventions might not always be successful, but the other person's chances of getting out from under that sin and the things that were impelling him or her into it are much greater with the help of such restorative intervention.

The church is not supposed to be a place where people can continue to sow to the flesh, or continue to live in destructive ways, without others getting involved and trying to get them back on course—just like Alcoholics Anonymous is not supposed to be a place where someone can go and keep drinking without an intervention. People go to AA meetings to stop drinking; Christians gather together in a church to stop living for themselves, to stop giving in to their self-centered impulses. And we *all* need one another's uninvited intervention from time to time if we are to stay on track. This is an important venue for the Spirit's intervention in our lives.

Prioritizing Reconciliation

A natural inclination of human beings is to hold grudges against people whom we believe to have wronged us. Many people have stories about neighbors, family members, or even members of churches who refuse to speak to or otherwise interact with one another on account of some real or imagined injury from the distant past. Paul believed that the Christian community was to be a community of forgiveness, of reconciliation:

---

4. The Greek word *praütēs* carries the sense of not being heavy-handed in dealing with a situation, not using all the force at one's disposal out of consideration for the other. See Walter Bauer, Frederick Danker, et al., *A Greek-English Lexicon of the New Testament and Other Early Christian Literature*, 3rd ed. (Chicago: University of Chicago Press, 2000), 861, col. 1.

> Don't grieve the Holy Spirit of God, with which you were sealed for the day of redemption. Let all bitterness and fuming and anger and clamoring and slander be lifted away from you, along with all malice. Be generous toward one another, well-disposed, forgiving each other just as God also forgave you in Christ. (Eph 4:30–31)

> Bear with one another, and if anyone has a complaint against someone, be gracious to one another. Just as the Lord was gracious toward you, so also you [should be gracious to one another]. (Col 3:13)

Christians were not encouraged to wink at injuries done to one another, but neither would Paul permit Christians to allow injuries to fester. Tempers might flare up because two people want to have things go different ways in the church, but these could not be allowed to create rifts. Unforgiveness is a cancer in Christ's body, and it needs to be excised with all due diligence and swiftness.

Sometimes we need to help reconciliation move forward; sometimes we need help with reconciliation ourselves. The charge to third parties is not to take sides, to start garnering support for one person over against the other, or even to start fighting among themselves over who's right and who's wrong, but rather to assist in the task of reconciliation: "I urge Euodia and I urge Syntyche to agree together in the Lord. And I ask you also, loyal partner, to help these women, who contended alongside me for the gospel with Clement and the rest of my coworkers, whose names are in the Book of Life" (Phil 4:2–3). Paul himself intervenes in a relationship gone bad between Euodia and Syntyche, and he asks his anonymous "loyal partner" also to help them come to a place of reconciliation.[5] In every church Paul still needs "loyal partners" who

---

5. Some scholars suggest that the Greek word translated "loyal partner"—*syzygos*—was actually a personal name. In a world where little girls received names like Euodia and Syntyche, it is not unthinkable that parents would saddle some poor little boy with a name like Syzygos, but no extrabiblical evidence has yet been found to suggest that "Syzygos" was in use as a proper name, though it is frequently used elsewhere in literature to address or describe a comrade or partner in some labor (see Bauer, Danker, et al., *Greek–English Lexicon*, 954, col. 2).

will help those sisters and brothers who are harboring resentment and unforgiveness to let it go and find reconciliation together.

Sharing Like Family

The early church was known for its liberal sharing of resources among its members. Christians shared what they had with one another, as any had need, as one would expect to see only among one's closest family members or in the most committed of friendships (as seen, for example, in Aristotle's famous maxim that "friends own all things in common").[6]

When the Christians in Jerusalem were in dire economic need, Paul took up a collection among all his largely Gentile Christian churches for their relief as an expression of their transformed relationship: Jews and Gentiles were now one family and would act toward one another as family. This was for Paul a sign of "the obedience that accompanies your confession of the gospel of Christ" (2 Cor 9:13).

> I do not mean that there should be relief for others and pressure on you, but it is a question of a fair balance between your present abundance and their need, so that their abundance may be for your need, in order that there may be a fair balance. As it is written, "The one who had much did not have too much, and the one who had little did not have too little." (2 Cor 8:13–15 NRSV; quoting Exod 16:18)

Paul's reference to the story of the gathering of manna is significant. During the wandering in the desert, God provided manna for the people's *daily* needs. Whatever was gathered beyond the day's need and hoarded turned to worms by the next morning (see Exod 16:14–21).

Paul invites his converts to view their own wealth in essentially this way: all that the Church universal gathers today is for the needs of the Church as a whole, to be shared throughout the global community as one great family at one great table, not squirreled away for our private consumption tomorrow, next year, or long into retirement. The only

---

6. Aristotle, *Nicomachean Ethics* 8.9.1 (1159b31–32).

reason we can't embrace such a view of our own wealth freely, I believe, is that we don't trust the Church universal to provide for our needs tomorrow in the way that Paul would have us—who have gathered much—provide for its needs today. While it is beyond the scope of the present work to treat this topic fully, let it suffice to say that sharing our resources makes our love real to sisters and brothers whose need can be relieved by the same. It makes the idea of the *family* of God real to them, and Paul calls us to allow God to transform our global Christian community in that direction.

Investing in and Encouraging One Another

In a world where people share largely superficial conversations, Paul calls the Church to be different. In 1 Thessalonians he twice asks his converts to keep encouraging one another on the basis of their shared faith and vision, nurtured by his teachings. In the face of grief over sisters and brothers who have died without seeing the fulfillment of the Christian hope, Paul speaks of how both those who are dead and those who are alive will share in the life of the resurrection at Christ's coming. He concludes: "So then, keep encouraging one another with these words" (1 Thess 4:18). Similarly, after reminding them about the importance of remaining vigilant and living as people who expect to encounter God, he concludes: "Therefore keep encouraging one another and building one another up, each one the other, just as you are doing" (1 Thess 5:11).

Paul calls churches to become communities that reinforce for one another the promises and the hope that we have in Christ so that we are individually better able to keep these promises in view and therefore live *for* those promises and *in* that hope. Many of the compromises we make in our discipleship, the side paths we take on this journey of transformation, happen because we are distracted by other promises and seek to satisfy our longings with other hopes—and the world around us is happy to keep dangling those before our eyes as bids for our servitude. This means investment in one another, for it takes time, it takes honesty, it takes prioritizing our relationships in the family of God.

Moving from Self-Centered Rights to Other-Centered Restraint

There is yet another point at which Paul's understanding of the kind of community the Spirit is seeking to form is markedly at odds with the kind of person whom Western culture in general, and American culture in particular, tends to nurture. We are very much attuned to our rights — what it is our "right" to do, to enjoy, to have. We tend to chafe against anything that impinges on our rights. There is an inherent conflict between the self-centered system of "rights" and the other-centered system of "obligations."

Paul faced situations in his churches where some individuals were claiming that they had a right to engage in certain kinds of behavior and to enjoy certain kinds of social interactions. These largely had to do with going to the kinds of dinners and parties where the host would serve meat from animals previously sacrificed to idols. (A good deal of meat in the city market came from sacrificial animals sold to the market butchers by the local temples.) Some Christians, however, had serious scruples about this kind of activity, since they were themselves "recovering idolaters." It bruised their conscience to see fellow Christians engage in it, but it seems they were also tempted to go further than their own consciences would permit them because of both the example and the scorn of those same Christians.

> "All things are lawful," but not all things are beneficial. "All things are lawful," but not all things build up. Do not seek your own advantage, but that of the other. ... Give no offense to Jews or to Greeks or to the church of God, just as I try to please everyone in everything I do, not seeking my own advantage, but that of many, so that they may be saved. (1 Cor 10:23-24, 32-33 NRSV)

> Let us ... no longer pass judgment on one another, but resolve instead never to put a stumbling block or hindrance in the way of another. I know and am persuaded in the Lord Jesus that nothing is unclean in itself; but it is unclean for anyone who thinks it unclean. If your brother or sister is being injured by what you eat, you are no longer

> walking in love. Do not let what you eat cause the ruin
> of one for whom Christ died. ... Let us then pursue what
> makes for peace and for mutual upbuilding. Do not, for
> the sake of food, destroy the work of God. Everything is
> indeed clean, but it is wrong for you to make others fall by
> what you eat; it is good not to eat meat or drink wine or do
> anything that makes your brother or sister stumble. (Rom
> 14:13–15, 19–21 NRSV)

Paul doesn't argue about whether or not it is a Christian's *right* to enjoy some particular experience or engage in some particular behavior.
Let it be granted that God is comfortable with our doing a great many
things that our fellow Christians may not be comfortable with our doing.
But Paul does insist that the enjoyment or exercise of our rights is not
the highest value in the community of Christ's body. Rather, assessing
the impact of our actions upon the sisters and brothers around us, and
choosing to do what will best serve their needs, is the highest value.

Paul's directives to his congregations are derived from his conviction
that, if Christ is indeed coming to life in individual believers, then the
mind that was in Christ must be evident in the actions of the various
parts of his body. That mind was set on relinquishing his own rights and
claims in the service of others and specifically in the service of God's
purposes for others. In his letter to his friends in Philippi, Paul urges
his converts to adopt Christ's mind-set in their dealings with one another. Christ's own example (see Phil 2:5-11) undergirds the main point of
Paul's advice: "Do nothing from selfish ambition or conceit, but in humility regard others as better than yourselves. Let each of you look not
to your own interests, but to the interests of others" (Phil 2:3-4 NRSV).

It takes this humility to put the faith journeys of other Christians
ahead of everything else we want to do, the many things we think so
important. It takes humility to seek reconciliation where pride would
feed rifts and resentment. It takes looking out for the interests of others
rather than our own to set aside our rights for the sake of another's peace,
or to invest our resources in another's present need rather than to save
it for some future need of our own. As Christ comes to life in each one
of us, the community of faith is transformed into his well-functioning

body, moved harmoniously by his one mind. This in turn becomes a means of grace assisting each one of us to persevere in his or her own journey of transformation, till we stand before God looking like the righteous one who has taken shape within us.

Breaking through Ethnic Barriers, Classes, Castes, and Gender Lines

A human society draws many lines to define its boundaries and its internal hierarchies and order. I took my family to Germany for a year in 2006. It was the first time our younger two sons flew. The youngest remarked in surprise that the states weren't actually different colors like on the maps around the house. From the sky, and I suspect from God's throne, the boundaries between states and countries aren't really all that marked or important. They are important to *our* maps and *our* mental conceptions of who makes up "us" and who makes up "them," who is a friend and who is an enemy, who is an equal and who is an inferior or even a superior. Paul is adamant that the Church is to be a place where we value one another and respond to one another according to the lines that *God* is drawing—and erasing—and not according to the lines we had been taught to see by our society. Which earth do Christians inhabit as their primary world? Are we in the first place, for example, Americans with other Americans, most of whom live within the borders of America marked out on the globe, or are we in the first place Christians with other Christians, who live all across the globe and who constitute, in God's sight, a single sovereign kingdom?

There was a great deal of mutual prejudice and antagonism between Jews and non-Jews in the first century. Jews looked upon non-Jews as ignorant, godless, and sinners by nature; centuries of Gentile domination of Israel did not help. Gentiles looked upon Jews as intolerant, superstitious, impious toward the gods of every other nation ("atheism" is, ironically, a charge often thrown at the Jewish community), and standoffish in the extreme. While there were Jews who admired facets of Greek culture and non-Jews who admired the austerity and morality of the Jewish people, they were more the exception.[7]

Paul saw God, therefore, doing something radically transformative of these relationships in Christ. He fought hard throughout his ministry to make sure that the old prejudices and boundaries did not pervert what he believed God was trying to do in this new people, the Church:

> For he is our peace; in his flesh he has made both groups into one and has broken down the dividing wall, that is, the hostility between us. He has abolished the law with its commandments and ordinances, that he might create in himself one new humanity in place of the two, thus making peace, and might reconcile both groups to God in one body through the cross, thus putting to death that hostility through it. (Eph 2:11–16 NRSV)

The Church was a place for the transformation of relationships between hostile groups, the wall of hostility being demolished and a new united community being formed out of the two, "being built together into a dwelling for God in the Spirit" (Eph 2:22). It was this interest in seeing this boundary transformed appropriately in the one body of Christ that lay behind Paul's rebuke of Peter in Antioch (Gal 2:11–14) as well as his resistance against the reintroduction of this boundary into the churches in Galatia. This unity represented a major shift in the religious and

---

7. Helpful works on this topic include Emilio Gabba, "The Growth of Anti-Judaism or the Greek Attitude towards Jews," in *The Cambridge History of Judaism*, ed. W. D. Davies and Louis Finkelstein, vol. 2, *The Hellenistic Age* (Cambridge: Cambridge University Press, 1989), 614–56; J. M. G. Barclay, *Jews in the Mediterranean Diaspora* (Edinburgh: T&T Clark, 1996), 181–228, 361–80. Barclay (*Mediterranean Diaspora*, 402–44) also provides a sketch of Diaspora Jewish practice foregrounding those elements that practically reinforced difference and thereby facilitated resentment. A comprehensive sourcebook for ancient anti- and philo-Judaism is Louis H. Feldman and Meyer Reinhold, eds., *Jewish Life and Thought among Greeks and Romans* (Minneapolis: Fortress, 1996). For an overview of the mutual prejudice between Jews and Gentiles in the Hellenistic and Roman periods, see David A. deSilva, *Apocrypha* (Core Biblical Studies; Nashville: Abingdon, 2012), 95–108.

social landscape, since Jews could claim scriptural authority for the lines that separated them from the other nations.[8]

Paul called other socially determined roles and lines of differentiation into question as well, affirming that God was seeking to transform these relationships in the new community.

> There is no longer a Jew or a Greek; there is no longer
> a slave or a free person; there is not "male and female":
> for you are all one in Christ Jesus. (Gal 3:28)

> Here there is not a Greek and a Jew, circumcision and lack
> of circumcision, a barbarian, a Scythian, a slave, a free
> person, but Christ is all things and in everything. (Col 3:11)

Slave labor was the bedrock of the Roman economy. It is estimated that one out of every five people living in Rome—and a higher percentage throughout the empire as a whole—fell into the category of being classified as a "living tool," to use Aristotle's definition of a slave, whether by birth into slavery, sale into slavery because of debt, or by new military conquest or suppression of revolt.[9] But, as freed slave George Teamoh titled his autobiography, *God Made Man, Man Made the Slave,*[10] and in the new community in Christ people would see one another and receive one another as *God* made them and was *re*making them, not as other humans had branded them.

Paul brings this home for one congregation and one household in his letter to Philemon. Onesimus' birth into the household of God as a son means he cannot be seen and treated any longer as a slave in Philemon's household, if Philemon is to be true to his *own* identity as a son in God's household:

---

8. The Jewish practice of making distinctions between clean and unclean animals was understood to be a reflection of God's action in making a distinction between Israel, which would be clean for God's use and association, and the remaining nations, which were unclean and unfit for God's association (see Lev 20:22–26). Indeed the call to Israel to "be holy, for I am holy" (Lev 11:44; see also Lev 11:45; 19:2; 20:7) included the necessity of observing the boundaries God created and affirmed: "I have separated you from the peoples" (Lev 20:24 NRSV).

9. Everett Ferguson, *Backgrounds of Early Christianity*, 2nd ed. (Grand Rapids: Eerdmans, 1993), 56. The quotation from Aristotle is from his *Politics*, 1.4 (1253b27–33).

10. F. N. Boney, Richard L. Hume, and Rafia Zafar, eds., *God Made Man, Man Made the Slave: The Autobiography of George Teamoh* (Macon, GA: Mercer University Press, 1992), 100.

> Perhaps this is why he was separated from you for a lit-
> tle while, in order that you might have him for eternity,
> no longer as a slave, but as more than a slave—a beloved
> brother, greatly so to me, and how much more so to you,
> both in the flesh and in the Lord? (Phlm 15–16)

The details of Onesimus' situation are unclear; what is clear is that Paul challenged Philemon to live out of their new relationship as two brothers in the Lord and not out of their old relationship of owner and slave in the world's economy.

Paul would challenge us to examine our congregations in light of this vision. A church that lives out its calling to be a transformed community will not be a community in which the lines drawn between ethnic groups, between people of different nationalities, between management and labor, professional and under- or unemployed, snowbirds and homeless have greater weight than the large circle God has drawn around everyone who belongs to Jesus. On the contrary it will be a counter-community in which people are valued—and enjoy the experience of being valued—not by their location in the world's matrix of status and worth, but wholly in accordance with their identity in Jesus, their place in God's family, and their contribution to the ongoing work of transformation in themselves, the church, and the world.

Hence Paul calls Christians to lavish honor on one another, and to take special care not to shame our sisters and brothers in Christ on the basis of anything that proceeds from their temporary, worldly status and circumstances (e.g., Rom 12:10, 16; 1 Cor 11:20–22). It will be a community whose members do not respond to a visiting Hispanic family by wondering whether they are in the country illegally, but by embracing them as family in Christ. It will be a community that anticipates that God can work as powerfully and significantly through a woman as through a man. We experience less of God's transforming power where we do not seek this reconciliation across walls of hostility among the people of God in Christ (whether racial, ethnic/national, socioeconomic, or patriarchal).

No Room for Partisanship

Paul sought to nurture Christian unity, apparently a challenge even before the proliferation of denominations. I have myself spent a good number of years working with churches of four different denominations—Episcopal, Assemblies of God, Lutheran, and United Methodist. I can't say that any *one* of them is the true Church of God. I *can* say that the Word was faithfully preached in every *one* of them, that the means of grace were duly offered and available, and that God was at work in and through many of the people in each congregation, just as his work was resisted by some. I *can* say that each one had a firm handle on the gospel, even if those handles were placed differently, so to speak, *on* the gospel; each reflected a vibrant facet of worship, discipleship, and service.

It is difficult to know precisely how Paul would confront the modern situation of denominationalism. During Paul's ministry, however, people *did* have their favorite preachers, and there were at least two major denominations—the Jewish-Christian church that was not so very open to people who did not follow a Torah-observant life, and a more assorted mass of Jewish-Christian, Gentile-Christian, and mixed churches that no longer defined the people of God in terms of Torah observance. Paul opposed *both* kinds of incipient denominationalism. The believers in Corinth, for example, tended to be highly partisan toward their favorite preacher or teacher, forming subgroups or factions within the church on this basis.

> Each of you says, "I belong to Paul," or "I belong to Apollos," or "I belong to Cephas," or "I belong to Christ." ... As long as there is jealousy and quarreling among you, are you not of the flesh, and behaving according to human inclinations? For when one says, "I belong to Paul," and another, "I belong to Apollos," are you not merely human? What then is Apollos? What is Paul? Servants through whom you came to believe, as the Lord assigned to each. (1 Cor 1:12; 3:3–4 NRSV)

The situation is considerably more complex nineteen centuries later, but one can still hear the fundamental parallels: "I am of Wesley," "I am of Luther," "I am of Calvin," and one smart aleck trying to trump everyone else, "I am of Christ." Denominations can be very good things; denominational *partisanship* is not. The impulses to affirm our group's ways as better, as more legitimate in the sight of God, are very basic, human impulses—but they come from the flesh rather than the Spirit. We could instead learn to appreciate the fact that different parts of Christ's body have discovered—and hold up for the other parts—facets of the gospel, of life in Christ, and of God's mission in the world that others may have missed. We could remember, with appropriate humility, that "we now see things reflected in an imperfect mirror" and only "then"—on the other side of death and the judgment—"we will see face-to-face" (1 Cor 13:12).

Denominational partisanship is a stain on the Church's honor in the eyes of outsiders. A colleague in Sri Lanka shared with me that the presence of multiple, rival denominations and smaller Christian groups there was one of the greatest hindrances to the Church's witness: "Why should we listen to you about leaving behind the religion of our fathers and mothers when you can't even agree among yourselves about your message?" We could probably hear similar testimonies in our own communities in the United States.

We have to allow that God tolerates a much greater diversity of practice than we, poor humans, tend to be able to accommodate in our own minds. *We* need to be right; those who do otherwise need to be *wrong*. Those who baptize their infants and those who don't, preferring to reserve the water till a person can make a profession of faith, can't both be right, can they? Paul writes:

> Some believe in eating anything, while the weak eat only vegetables. Those who eat must not despise those who abstain, and those who abstain must not pass judgment on those who eat; for God has welcomed them. Who are you to pass judgment on servants of another? It is before their own lord that they stand or fall. And they will be upheld, for the Lord is able to make them stand. Some judge one day to be better than another, while others judge all days to be alike. Let all be fully convinced in their own minds.

> Those who observe the day, observe it in honor of the Lord.
> Also those who eat, eat in honor of the Lord, since they give
> thanks to God; while those who abstain, abstain in honor
> of the Lord and give thanks to God. (Rom 14:2-6 NRSV)

There are many areas in which different, even conflicting, practices
may be equally "right" in God's estimation, because they are done in the
Spirit. They are done with the intention *and* the result of honoring God.
We should observe that, in this passage, Paul addresses two points of difference in practice for which one side had stronger scriptural support.
Jewish Christians would have tended to avoid eating meat unless they
could be assured that it was from an animal that had been killed in the
proper way and that had not been involved in a sacrifice to another god.
They would also have been more insistent concerning the observance
of a particular day for honoring God, namely the Sabbath. Paul affirms
both *their* practice and the *contrary* practices as equally acceptable in
God's sight where the intent and result is the same: God is honored in
what God's people are doing.

If Christian community is to be different from worldly-minded communities, many of us may need to grow in toleration of different practices rather than condemn those who have different Christian practices as
inferior, ignorant, or even unfaithful. It is worth pondering some common points of division, disagreement, even hostility between Christian
bodies and asking how Paul, who affirmed a variety of God-pleasing
practices in regard to observing or not observing the Sabbath or dietary
laws so clearly supported in the Torah, would address the variety found
among Christian denominations and individuals in regard to:

- the drinking of wine or other alcoholic beverages
- social dancing
- infant baptism or waiting until the time of "decision"
- baptism by immersion (forward? backward? with what spoken formula?) or pouring or sprinkling
- formal, liturgical worship or a more relaxed service style
- veneration of the saints

- the size of the OT canon
- charismatic expressions of devotion in public worship (e.g., raising one's hands, speaking or praying in tongues, spontaneous praise)
- worship on Saturday versus Sunday
- observing or not observing the liturgical calendar
- the number of sacraments, if any

I do not say that Paul's words in Romans apply to *everything*—Paul drew clear boundaries around, thus defining the limits of, Christian practice as well. But I do suspect that Paul's words promoting toleration apply to a great many things concerning which we have strong preferences and convictions. And we cannot allow our preferences and convictions to become walls of division within Christ's body.

Christian Families within the Christian Family

The early Christian movement involved not simply individual converts but in many cases entire households that had converted to the new faith. We read, for example, of the conversions of the households of Cornelius (Acts 10:34, 47–48), Lydia (Acts 16:15), the Philippian jailer (Acts 16:27–34), Stephanas of Corinth (1 Cor 1:16), and Onesiphorus (2 Tim 1:16; 4:19). The conversion of the household as a whole typically followed on the decision of the head of the household to join the Christian movement. In a very practical way the movement depended on natural households and the willingness of Christian householders to extend hospitality to the local congregation so that it would have a place to meet (Rom 16:3–5, 23; 1 Cor 16:19; Phlm 2), and to traveling teachers and delegates of the churches (Rom 16:1–2; Col 4:10; Phlm 22).

The natural household was typically conceived of as an authoritarian, male-led social unit. Aristotle would speak of household management (in Greek, *oikonomia*, whence our English "economy") as concerned with "the rule of a master over slaves, ... of a father [over children], and ... of a husband [over a wife]," the same man being invested with the greater authority in each set of paired relationships

(*Pol.* 1.12 [1259a36–39]). Ethicists urged that this authority be exercised with duty, diligence, and beneficent care, moderating particularly the authority of the husband over the wife as that of a senior over a junior partner or a permanently elected official over a fellow citizen (Aristotle, *Pol.* 1.12 [1259b6–10]), but the hierarchy was absolute. In practice, heads of households wore their authority in a manner reflective of their own virtue or lack thereof.[11]

Paul has a great deal to say about living together not just as the larger Christian family but as Christian *families* as well. Perhaps the most important point here is that we make a mistake when we look only to the so-called household codes of Eph 5:21–6:4 and Col 3:18–4:1 for guidance in this area. Despite an awareness that he is addressing congregations in which multiple (complete) households are also to be found, Paul actually says very little that is specific to these natural relationships.[12] Christian families are called to shape themselves in accordance with the overarching guidelines for *all* Christian community, which must also pertain to the community within Christian households, with passages such as the household codes offering *additional* counsel, not *exclusive* guidance. Thus the starting point for the transformed relationships within the household would not be the household codes, per se, but instructions such as:

> Have a common mind, holding the same love, keeping your souls in harmony, agreeing, doing nothing from a desire to promote your agenda over others' or from too high an opinion of yourselves, but, in humility considering one another to be of higher dignity than yourselves,

---

11. Further on the household in the Graeco-Roman world, see deSilva, *Honor, Patronage, Kinship & Purity*, 173–93; Halvor Moxnes, ed., *Constructing Early Christian Families* (London: Routledge, 1997); Carolyn Osiek and David Balch, *Families in the New Testament World: Households and House Churches* (Louisville: Westminster John Knox, 1997).

12. Indeed, if Ephesians and Colossians prove to have been written by Paul's surviving team members rather than the apostle himself, Paul says almost *nothing* about relationships within the Christian household except what he applies to all relationships between Christians. I am myself of the opinion that Colossians is certainly genuine, and Ephesians quite possibly so (see David A. deSilva, *An Introduction to the New Testament: Contexts, Methods & Ministry Formation* [Downers Grove, IL: InterVarsity Press, 2004], 696–701, 716–21).

> looking each of you not to what is in your own interest,
> but to what is in the other's interest. (Phil 2:2–4)

> Don't use your freedom as an opportunity to gratify your
> self-centered impulses, but serve one another as slaves
> through love. (Gal 5:13)

This position is supported by the seamless way in which Paul segues from instructions to all Christians into relationship-specific instruction in Ephesians:

> Don't get drunk on wine, which is wastefulness, but be
> filled with the Spirit,
> (19) reciting psalms and hymns and spiritual songs to
> one another, singing and making music in your heart to
> the Lord,
> (20) giving thanks to God the Father at all times and for
> everything in the name of our Lord Jesus Christ,
> (21) being submissive to one another out of respect
> for Christ:
> (22) the wives to their own husbands as to the Lord, be-
> cause the husband is the wife's head as even Christ is the
> church's head, he being the Savior of the body.
> (Eph 5:18–23)

I have provided a structural translation to demonstrate the essential point: the instructions to Christian wives within Christian households, and thus the entire series of household codes to follow, proceeds in an integral and organically connected way from the instructions to the whole of the Christian community. The action of Eph 5:21 ("being sub-missive") is syntactically dependent on the material that precedes, but the action of Eph 5:22 is even more fully dependent on the preceding material since, without 5:21, there is no verbal action in 5:22. Thus trans-lations that interject a paragraph heading after 5:21 and 5:22 (like the ESV and HCSB) are dividing asunder what Paul has carefully joined together, carefully embedding the wife's submission to her husband in the larg-er Christian ethos of mutual, other-centered submission. This larger ethos is just as transformative of the husband's exercise of his authority within the Christian household as Paul's introduction of the example of Christ's use of his authority as the pattern for the husband. Translations that, perhaps less objectionably, interject a paragraph heading prior to 5:21 (like the NRSV and NIV) are also introducing a syntactically inappropriate division, however, as 5:21 is not merely the introduction to the household codes but also the conclusion to Paul's general words of instruction to the entire Christian community.[13]

The instructions given to Christian slaves and masters are even more striking and subversive of the exercise of authority as conceived outside the Christian community:

> Slaves, obey your earthly masters with fear and trembling, in singleness of heart, as you obey Christ; not only while being watched, and in order to please them, but as slaves of Christ, doing the will of God from the heart. Render service with enthusiasm, as to the Lord and not to men and women, knowing that whatever good we do, we will receive the same again from the Lord, whether we are slaves or free.
>
> And, masters, do the same to them. Stop threatening them, for you know that both of you have the same Master in heaven, and with him there is no partiality. (Eph 6:5–9 NRSV)

The instructions given to slaves are admittedly not transformative of the relationship, though Paul does introduce an important qualifier in 6:8, indicating that the status of being "slave" or "free" does not affect how the Lord will look upon and respond to the individual. This is reflected as well in the following verse, notably another witness to God's distance from all partiality. These are clear reminders, as noted already, that God made human beings, but human beings introduced the distinction between slave and free person, with the result that this distinction carries no weight before God and the institution itself cannot

---

13. The CEB is noteworthy in this regard for setting off Eph 5:15–6:9 as a single section.

claim divine legitimation or authority. What is transformative is the instruction given to Christian masters, which is simply, "do the same for them." If one bothers to search for an antecedent here that might define what this "same" constitutes, one will come upon the commands to "render service as a slave (*douleuontes*, 6:7) with a glad heart," mindful that the Lord looks on to evaluate and repay our actions. This is a bold move in the direction of transforming the relationship as defined by the Graeco-Roman world—the relationship of a "master" to a "living tool" is subsumed under the relationship of brothers and sisters who are to "be submissive to one to another" (Eph 5:21) or are to "serve one another as slaves out of love" (Gal 5:13). The overarching point of the household codes themselves seems to be that relationships within the (traditionally authoritarian) household *must* be transformed in terms of the larger, general ethos of Christian community.

Conclusion

Bringing into being a community of this character was part of the "good news" of Paul's gospel. A group of people committed to one another's progress in the transformation God longed to work within them, sensitive to where each person is in terms of his or her faith and limitations, reflective of how God values each as a son or daughter independent of the social categories into which that person was born or into which he or she fell, ready to support each member at his or her places of need like family—how could the invitation to become part of such a community *not* have been "good news" to the people to whom Paul announced the gospel? And how could it not be "good news" to the people around us in our churches, and beyond our churches, to the extent that we allow God's Spirit to transform us in these ways?

By this point it is probably also clear that we *can only* become the new persons God is changing us to become in Christ in the context of our interactions with one another and particularly in our interactions as congregations. In the early part of the third century, Origen had declared "Outside of this house, that is, outside the Church, no one is saved" (*Homilies on Joshua* 3:5). While the Roman Catholic doctrine of *extra ecclesiam nulla salus* ("no salvation outside the Church"), of which a statement such as Origen's was a precursor, has occasioned no small controversy, Origen's statement speaks to a practical reality of which we too easily lose sight in our individualistic culture. My transformation depends upon my living in community with a group of people committed to the same transformation in themselves and in me, where I can practice the new behaviors and grow the new heart of the new person God seeks to nurture within me, so that I can become a person who is righteous in his sight, a person in whom he sees his Son, Jesus.

CHAPTER 4

The Gospel Means the Transformation of the Cosmos: You Are Free from the World's Rules to Witness to God's Rule

P aul understands the scope of God's "good news" to encompass not only the individual and the community of faith but the cosmos itself—at least the "cosmos" conceived as the present ordering of the world and even the present terrestrial sphere.[1] Transformation is not simply a matter of individual Christians changing their attitudes and behaviors within the existing structures of society. It's a matter of the transformation Christ seeks to make in our individual and collective lives also breaking out of the limitations imposed by "the way things are done" in society at every level and in every area of our existence

---

1. N. T. Wright is correct therefore to question the self-centered soteriology to which many theologians, professional and lay, limit themselves: "The theological equivalent of supposing that the sun goes round the earth is the belief that the whole of Christian truth *is all about me and my salvation.* ... God is not circling around us. We are circling around him. ... God made humans for a purpose: not simply for themselves, not simply so that they could be in relationship with him, but so that *through* them, as his image-bearers, he could bring his wise, glad, fruitful order to the world" (*Justification: God's Plan and Paul's Vision* [Downers Grove, IL: InterVarsity Press, 2009], 23–24). God's plan has always been bigger than individual souls.

and practice. Salvation, in other words, is not just a matter of individual and communal transformation but systemic transformation as well—though this latter will not be complete until Christ brings an end to all current authorities and powers in this world and institutes the fullness of the kingdom of God.

As Christians move out of the structures of "this age" and organize their lives and their communities around new principles and structures grounded in Christ's teachings and the vision for human community articulated throughout the NT, they accomplish three things. They declare the temporary nature of the ordering of "this age"; they invite broader critical reflection on its normally unquestioned structures; and they bear witness to the larger transformation yet to come and even bring that larger transformation—if only in the way of hints and foretastes—into reality.

The "World" as Problem

When talking about Paul's understanding of how the good news affects "the world" and positions believers to respond to "the world," it is important always to inquire into the sense of "the world" in any given instance. Paul generally speaks of "the world" using two terms: *kosmos* and *aiōn*. The Greek–English lexicon that comes as close to an "industry standard" among NT scholars identifies eight distinct lexical senses to the Greek word *kosmos*, given here with their typical translational glosses following in italics:

1. that which serves to beautify through decoration, *adornment, adorning*

2. condition of orderliness, *orderly arrangement, order*

3. the sum total of everything here and now, *the world, the (orderly) universe*

4. the sum total of all beings above the level of the animals, *the world*

5. planet earth as a place of inhabitation, *the world*

6. humanity in general, *the world*

7.   the system of human existence in its many aspects, *the world*

8.   collective aspect of an entity, *totality, sum total*[2]

We need to be particularly concerned with three basic senses and Paul's evaluation of the "world" in each sense: (1) the "world" as the space within which both saving activity and sin happen is essentially neutral; (2) the "world" as a system of priorities, logic, boundaries, and practices that people inherit by virtue of being born into a society is essentially hostile to God's purposes and vision; (3) the "world" as metonym for its inhabitants. "World" in the third sense can be neutral or hostile, depending on whether Paul is stressing these inhabitants' immersion in the way of thinking, valuing, and relating named in the second sense.

While the second term, *aiōn*, is often rendered in English as "world," it is more properly rendered as "age" (as in an "epoch" or a period of time). In particular the term is often used in the context of a contrast, explicit or implicit, between "this age," by which Paul means the present state of the cosmos between the fall and the renewal of all things, and "the coming age" or "coming ages," by which Paul points ahead to the new ordering of existence in the kingdom of God.[3] The concept of a sequence of ages or epochs, the present one being an age of evil or imperfection and a coming one being an age in which God's good purposes for his people and, indeed, all of creation will be fulfilled, is a staple of Jewish apocalyptic thought—the larger conceptual matrix within which Paul's own theology took shape.[4] That Paul thinks of *kosmos* (in some senses) and the present *aiōn* as essentially synonymous is evident from several passages in his writings. For example, he warns the Corinthians: "Do not deceive yourselves. If you think that you are wise in this age (*aiōn*), you should become fools so that you

---

2. Walter Bauer, Frederick Danker, et al., *A Greek-English Lexicon of the New Testament and Other Early Christian Literature*, 3rd ed. (Chicago: University of Chicago Press, 2000), 561–63.
3. Compare Galatians 1:4, where Paul speaks of "this present, evil age," with Gal 1:5, where he speaks of God's glory enduring into "the ages of ages," that is, the eternity that succeeds this corrupted age. A similar distinction is made in Eph 1:21 as well as Eph 2:1–2, 7.
4. A pioneering work in this regard is J. Christiaan Beker, *Paul the Apostle: The Triumph of God in Life and Thought* (Philadelphia: Fortress, 1980). See also his *Paul's Apocalyptic Gospel: The Coming Triumph of God* (Philadelphia: Fortress, 1982) and the abridged version of *Paul the Apostle* published as *The Triumph of God: The Essence of Paul's Gospel* (Minneapolis: Fortress, 1990).

may become wise. For the wisdom of this world (*kosmos*) is foolish-ness with God" (1 Cor 3:18–19a NRSV). The present "age" is the period dominated by a certain "ordering" (*kosmos*) of affairs that is temporary, fallen, and, in God's estimation, folly.[5]

Paul identifies the logic, the values, the hierarchies, and the priori-ties of "this age," active in "the world" as a system around us, most fully as a problem in the opening chapters of 1 Corinthians:

> The message about the cross is foolishness to those who are perishing, but to us who are being saved it is the power of God. For it is written, "I will destroy the wis-dom of the wise, and the discernment of the discerning I will thwart." Where is the one who is wise? Where is the scribe? Where is the debater of this age? Has not God made foolish the wisdom of the world? For since, in the wisdom of God, the world did not know God through wis-dom, God decided, through the foolishness of our procla-mation, to save those who believe. For Jews demand signs and Greeks desire wisdom, but we proclaim Christ cruci-fied, a stumbling block to Jews and foolishness to Gentiles, but to those who are the called, both Jews and Greeks, Christ the power of God and the wisdom of God. For God's foolishness is wiser than human wisdom, and God's weak-ness is stronger than human strength. (1 Cor 1:18–25 NRSV)

> Do not deceive yourselves. If you think that you are wise in this age, you should become fools so that you may be-come wise. For the wisdom of this world is foolishness with God. (1 Cor 3:18–19a NRSV)

At the heart of this critique is the fundamental disconnect between the "wisdom" that undergirds and reinforces the systems operative in the societies of "this age" and the wisdom that comes from God (1:21). The

---

5. See also 1 Cor 1:20, where one finds a similar parallelism. The two terms are linked even more closely in a single phrase in Eph 2:1–2: "You were dead through the trespasses and sins in which you once lived, following the course (*aiōn*) of this world (*kosmos*), following the ruler of the power of the air, the spirit that is now at work among those who are disobedient" (NRSV).

former is built upon foundations that are not God's and are indeed incompatible with God's foundations (illustrated by the fact that the societies animated by "the wisdom of the world" are all idolatrous societies, alienated from God). A more developed statement of this theme appears in Rom 1:18–32, which itself builds upon Hellenistic Jewish thought in regard to Gentile piety and practice (see, for example, Wis 13:1–9; 14:22–31).

The cross as the focal point of divine revelation (1 Cor 1:18, 22–24) brings the problem of the world's "wisdom" forcefully into the open. Jesus is accounted, according to this "wisdom," a disgraced loser, an executed criminal, a nobody, a failure. But in God's estimation Jesus is the righteous one whom God exalts above every other living being; Jesus is the obedient one through whom God's good purposes are accomplished; Jesus is the supreme benefactor, whose death on behalf of others in debts all to himself (recall 2 Cor 5:15) and brings him the greatest honor in God's economy. The cross of Christ confronts the Torah with devastating effects on the latter (see Gal 3:10–14); it confronts the "wisdom of the world" with equally devastating effects, showing it to be empty and folly outside its own limited, closed, and temporary system (1:19–20).

Moreover, the path to deliverance and to "glory" involves embracing a life built on God's wisdom rather than the world's. In this context one cannot help but recall the words attributed to Jesus in Mark's Gospel:

> You know that among the Gentiles those whom they recognize as their rulers lord it over them, and their great ones are tyrants over them. But it is not so among you; but whoever wishes to become great among you must be your servant, and whoever wishes to be first among you must be slave of all. (Mark 10:42–44 NRSV)

According to the world's "wisdom," greatness or precedence comes from power over others and from the willingness or acquiescence of others to serve the greater one. The structures and systems of this age are built on this core conviction concerning value and power. The metaphorical use of the language of "up" and "down," "above" and "below," to speak about hierarchies of power, position, authority, and value encapsulates the inner and unquestioned logic of the world's wisdom in this regard. But this is all inverted in God's wisdom. Those who make themselves servants to others in the greatest degree are those who come out "first." Those who put themselves on the "bottom" are the ones who come out on "top" in God's estimation, showing the "wisdom of the world" to be turned completely on its head. Simply put, "down" is "up."[6] Paul captures this inversion of the world's logic and wisdom in the hymnic passage about Christ's voluntary self-abasement in service to others as the path to exaltation before God—commending this similarly as a model for Christ's followers (Phil 2:1-11).

The world's logic as encapsulated in the concepts and valuations of "up" and "down," and the pervasive, systemic incarnation of these concepts and valuations throughout human society, is one example of how the present age gives an "orderly arrangement" (*kosmos*) to human existence in society. The "orderly arrangement" of this present age, however, subjects human beings to virtual slavery to what Paul calls the *stoicheia tou kosmou* (Gal 4:1-11; Col 2:8, 20-22). This is a difficult concept to understand, let alone translate, but the *stoicheia* and their impact on human beings and human community are clearly a significant facet of what is wrong with the cosmos and what Christ came to remedy:

> And I say, for the extent of time that the heir is a minor, he or she differs in no way from a slave, even though he or she is master of all, but he or she is under guardians and stewards until the time set by the father. In this way, we also, when we were minors, were enslaved under the fundamental principles of the cosmos (*ta stoicheia tou kosmou*): But when the fullness of time came, God sent his son, coming into being from a woman, coming into being under Torah, in order to redeem those under Torah, in order that we might receive adoption as children. ... But formerly, not perceiving God, you were enslaved to things that were not gods by nature. And now, knowing

---

6. In a similar way, in regard to possessions, Jesus will claim that "giving away" really means "saving up," whereas "saving up" is actually throwing away (see Matt 6:19-21; 19:21; Luke 12:33-34; 18:22).

God—and, what is more, being known by God—how can you turn back again to the weak and impoverished elementary principles (*stoicheia*), to which you desire again to submit yourselves afresh as slaves?! You are observing days and months and seasons and years! I am afraid for you, lest somehow I have labored over you for nothing! (Gal 4:1–5, 8–11)

See to it that no one takes you captive through philosophy and empty deceit, according to human tradition, according to the elemental spirits of the universe (*ta stoicheia tou kosmou*), and not according to Christ. ... If with Christ you died to the elemental spirits of the universe (*ta stoicheia tou kosmou*), why do you live as if you still belonged to the world? Why do you submit to regulations, "Do not handle, Do not taste, Do not touch"? All these regulations refer to things that perish with use; they are simply human commands and teachings. (Col 2:8, 20–22 NRSV)

What are these *stoicheia tou kosmou*?[7] The term *stoicheia* can refer to a series of things lined up in a row, hence the alphabet, and in an extended sense to "the ABCs" of some body of teaching, even the "ABCs" of human and institutional logic as this has taken shape in our rebellion against God. Paul is not using this in a positive sense but rather to refer to the rules, ideas, values, prejudices, and divisive categories (like "slave versus free," "male versus female," "Greek versus barbarian," "Jew versus Greek") that imprison and constrain those who grow up knowing nothing else and nothing better. Slavery to the *stoicheia* is in this sense slavery to "the way the world works" in the sense of an uncritical acquiescence to the rules and parameters that the world around us sets on our lives.[8]

---

7. For a fuller treatment of this question, see David A. deSilva, *Global Readings: A Sri Lankan Commentary on Paul's Letter to the Galatians* (Eugene, OR: Wipf & Stock, 2011), 197–201 and the literature cited therein.
8. See J. Louis Martyn, *Galatians*, Anchor Bible (New York: Doubleday, 1997), 389, 404.

The best attested meaning for the phrase *stoicheia tou kosmou* in the first century and before is the elements out of which the natural world was believed to have been made, namely earth, water, air, and fire. These elements were often regarded as gods themselves or related to particular gods (see Philo, *Contempl.* 3; *Decal.* 53; Wis 13:1–2) and thus exercised spiritual force over the lives and actions of human beings. The term could also be applied to sun, moon, other stars, and planets, also held to exercise influence over people, whether in the form of a religious calendar (as among the Jews; see Gal 4:11, especially) or in the form of the Gentiles' obsession with horoscopes and the like. In these senses as well the *stoicheia* had a dimension of superhuman power, as the rules of "the way the world worked," the idol-permeated structures of society, and the astral powers confronted the pagan as irresistible forces calling for submission without question. It is noteworthy that Paul regards the Torah itself to be on a par with the *stoicheia tou kosmou* in terms of its power as a constraining, enslaving force.

There is a sense in which the *stoicheia tou kosmou* have a spiritual power and may even be taken to represent spiritual forces; there is also a sense that these *stoicheia* are manifested in the fundamental and usually unquestioned logic of any given human society, any way of ordering social reality. In "this present, evil age" (Gal 1:4), the *stoicheia* represent the guiding powers and principles of this age, the building blocks from which the present, evil age is composed and that have contributed to perverting and corrupting the present age.

It seems to me that the discussions in the modern context that come closest to naming the kinds of realities that Paul was trying to name using the phrase *stoicheia tou kosmou* are discussions of "systems of domination" that articulate and reinforce their own logic and practices, and are geared to move individuals toward achieving the goals set out by the system.[9] Militarism is one example. We assume uncritically and take it for granted that countries have to have active militaries and that national security depends on devoting a significant portion of the society's resources to maintaining the military and its goals (e.g., maintaining tactical superiority over other existing militaries). We assume fairly uncritically that the use of violence in defense of national interests, whether at home or abroad, is a reasonable strategy in the pursuit of peace and security. We never dare to imagine what our country might look like without a military and what could be accomplished at home and abroad for good with the resources we dedicate to maintaining the power to wage war. Now I readily grant that it may not be possible, in the end, to disband the military machine in a world where every country has a military machine—but this just serves to reinforce my point that militarism has become a self-perpetuating, self-sustaining system that imposes its own logic, its own rules about human interactions, its own priorities concerning the reasonable use of resources on any given population. And that logic, those rules, and those priorities are simply *not* the logic, rules, and priorities of the God of Jesus Christ.

Paul, alongside other early Christians, perceives that the "problem"—that state from which Christ liberates us—is bigger than individual sin, even bigger than a group's behavior. The problem is systemic; it pervades human societies; and it confronts and directs human beings with supernatural force. In only somewhat mythologizing language, Paul speaks of "powers" at work against God's rule and those who would align themselves with God's rule: "For our struggle is not against enemies of blood and flesh, but against the rulers, against the authorities, against the cosmic powers of this present darkness, against the spiritual forces of evil in the heavenly places" (Eph 6:12 NRSV). These "cosmic powers"

---

9. Some resources that I have found to be particularly helpful for thinking about the "powers and principalities" that constrain human society, the foundational logic of the world-gone-astray from God, include: C. Dale White, *Making a Just Peace: Human Rights and Domination Systems* (Nashville: Abingdon, 1998); Walter Wink, *Naming the Powers: The Language of Power in the New Testament* (Minneapolis: Fortress, 1984); ibid., *Unmasking the Powers: The Invisible Forces That Determine Human Existence* (Minneapolis: Fortress, 1986); ibid., *Engaging the Powers: Discernment and Resistance in a World of Domination* (Minneapolis: Fortress, 1992); Vinoth Ramachandra, *Subverting Global Myths: Theology and the Public Issues Shaping Our World* (Downers Grove, IL: InterVarsity Press, 2008).

may not be entities with personalities, but individuals encounter them nevertheless as forces beyond the individual, and in some regards as suprasocial forces, constraining personal choices and even imagination.

THE TRANSFORMATION OF OUR RELATIONSHIP TO THE *KOSMOS*

Sociologist Bryan Wilson described religious movements based on how a given movement's members expected the group's goals to be realized in this world.[10] Two relevant categories were the "reformist" and "revolutionary" approaches. The reformist group expects to accomplish God's purposes, in effect, by changing the structures of this world so that they and their effects are realigned with God's purposes for the world. The revolutionary group expects God's purposes to be accomplished only through a radical reordering and replacement of the structures of this world, whether indirectly through the group's intervention or through God's direct intervention in the course of human history.

We have already examined enough evidence to demonstrate that Paul was not inclined toward the "reformist" approach. Christians should themselves live and relate in new ways, but Paul did not regard this as a new weave that would change the fabric of society. Paul was also not revolutionist in the sense of expecting that Christ's followers would participate in the overthrow and replacement of the current ordering of the world. His attitude toward Roman authorities, expressed in writing in Rom 13, has become one of the firmest pillars for the secular authority in Christian Scripture:

> Let every person be subject to the governing authorities; for there is no authority except from God, and those authorities that exist have been instituted by God. Therefore whoever resists authority resists what God has appointed, and those who resist will incur judgment. For rulers are not a terror to good conduct, but to bad. Do you wish

---

10. Bryan Wilson, *Magic and the Millennium: A Sociological Study of Religious Movements of Protest among Tribal and Third-World Peoples* (New York: Harper & Row, 1973), 22–26. Not all of his categories are mutually exclusive, though the two discussed here are.

to have no fear of the authority? Then do what is good, and you will receive its approval; for it is God's servant for your good. But if you do what is wrong, you should be afraid, for the authority does not bear the sword in vain! It is the servant of God to execute wrath on the wrong-doer. Therefore one must be subject, not only because of wrath but also because of conscience. For the same reason you also pay taxes, for the authorities are God's servants, busy with this very thing. Pay to all what is due them— taxes to whom taxes are due, revenue to whom revenue is due, respect to whom respect is due, honor to whom honor is due. Owe no one anything, except to love one another; for the one who loves another has fulfilled the law. (Rom 13:1–8 NRSV)

There was a sense in which, Paul believed, the "ordering" of this world was still a vehicle for God's right ordering of human society. One is left to wonder how Paul's view might have changed once indeed the rulers *did* become "a terror to good conduct," once "doing what is good" in God's sight did indeed bring (capital) punishment rather than "approv-al." Paul wrote his letter to the Christians in Rome during the earlier years of Nero's reign (AD 51–64), while Nero was still under the tutelage and control of the philosopher-senator Seneca and the general Burrhus. After the brutalization of Christians in Rome (which traditionally in-cludes the martyrdoms of Paul and Peter) under Nero in his later years, Paul might well have taken a more critical position in regard to "human authorities" such as we find, for example, in John's critique of Roman power in Revelation.[11]

Paul was entirely revolutionist, however, insofar as he did look for-ward to the overthrow of all current human power arrangements and of

---

11. Paul's encounters with Roman power were admittedly not uniformly positive even prior to writing Romans. He had experienced punishment at the hands of Roman authorities (be-ing "beaten three times with rods" indicates a Roman punishment, 2 Cor 11:25), but he had apparently also experienced helpful interventions from Roman administration (Acts 18:12–16). On Revelation as resistance literature, see Nelson Kraybill, *Apocalypse and Allegiance: Worship, Politics, and Devotion in the Book of Revelation* (Grand Rapids: Brazos, 2010); David A. deSilva, *Unholy Allegiances: Heeding Revelation's Warning* (Peabody, MA: Hendrickson, 2013).

the Roman Empire itself at the coming of Jesus, who would hand "over the kingdom to God the Father, after he has destroyed every ruler and every authority and power" (1 Cor 15:24 NRSV). The rulers and authorities might serve God's ends in the present time, but they were temporary and destined for destruction in the not-too-distant future.[12] Indeed at one point he even mocks the Roman government's proclamation of "peace and security" as bald-faced self-deception (1 Thess 5:3).[13] Perhaps significantly, Paul closely follows his words counseling submission to the Roman authorities (Rom 13:1–7) with a reminder to his converts about the drawing near of the day of God's kingdom and their deliverance (Rom 13:11).

This revolution is coming, Paul says, and in several important ways he invites Christians to start living now as though the revolution has already happened and as though that part of the cosmos that is the Christian movement were already under new management. Several statements in Paul's letters point in this direction:

> [God] has rescued us from the power of darkness and transferred us into the kingdom of his beloved Son, in whom we have redemption, the forgiveness of sins. (Col 1:13–14 NRSV)

> But may it not be for me to boast, except in the cross of our Lord Jesus Christ, through which the cosmos has been crucified to me and I to the cosmos. For neither circumcision nor uncircumcision is anything, but a new creation— *now that's something.* (Gal 6:14–15)

> Don't allow yourselves to be fit into the schema and structures (*syschēmatizesthe*) of this age, but be transformed (*metamorphousethe*) as your minds are made new, in order

---

12. Compare also the milder statement in Col 2 concerning what God has already done to these same "rulers and authorities" in the cross of Jesus: "he disarmed the rulers and authorities and made a public example of them, triumphing over them in it" (Col 2:15 NRSV).

13. Roman authorities and supportive subjects spoke about the *pax Romana* or the *pax Augusti* as the stable and safe state established by Augustus and perpetuated under his successors. *Pax* and *Securitas* are among the more common deities or personifications featured on the reverse sides of Roman coins of the period.

> that you may be able to discern what is the good and pleas-
> ing and perfect will of God. (Rom 12:2)

> I mean, brothers and sisters, the appointed time has grown
> short; from now on, let even those who have wives be as
> though they had none, and those who mourn as though
> they were not mourning, and those who rejoice as though
> they were not rejoicing, and those who buy as though they
> had no possessions, and those who deal with the world as
> though they had no dealings with it. For the present form
> of this world is passing away. (1 Cor 7:29–31 NRSV)

The statement from Colossians is both a sweeping indictment of the
present world order and a declaration of a change in governance that
has already taken place. The challenge for Christians becomes, then,
to live in the midst of the "power of darkness" as citizens who order
their common and individual lives in line with the "kingdom of [the] beloved Son," that is, built on the foundations of his teaching and example.
The statement from Galatians declares a complete break between the
life of Paul (and by extension the life of the believer who walks in the
same direction of transformation as does Paul) and the structures, power, and foundational logic and priorities of the "cosmos" as manifested
especially in the domination of the *stoicheia tou kosmou*. Once again Paul
declares that what matters in God's sight is neither being in nor *not*
being in a circumcised state, and therefore part of a particular ethnic
group in this present age, but being part of the "new creation" that God
is bringing about, a creation that lives independently of and beyond the
kinds of distinctions the logic of this age forces upon human beings (see
once again, e.g., Gal 3:28). This is also the import of the exhortation from
Romans. The translation given above is rendered somewhat freely to
highlight the two options facing Christians—either to allow themselves
to continue to be squeezed into the molds and structures of this present,
evil age, or to break out of those molds and structures as they give more
and more of themselves and their lives together over to the transformation the Spirit of God is working in and among them. This "as if not"
way of living in this present world—living *as if* its business and its order
are *not* the ultimate and unchallengeable way of doing things, setting

the direction in which people ought to occupy themselves—becomes a living witness to its temporary nature, that "the present form of this world is passing away."

In all the areas of life open to such reconstruction, Christians are set free to—and even positively urged to—divest themselves of the arrangements and structures that do not make sufficient room for living out the values of the kingdom and the directives of the gospel. Instead they are to create new arrangements and structures that *do* facilitate these values and directives. Paul himself shows something of this at work as he promotes his revolutionary conception of the "household of God," leading to revolutionary practices. One of the most striking of these practices is the circumvention of the master-slave relationship (a social structure imposed on human beings by the *stoicheia* undergirding Roman imperialism) by claiming that a Christian master and a Christian slave become brothers or sisters in the "new creation" that Christ is bringing about. Thus they can no longer view or treat each other on the basis of the old relationship (Phlm 15–16), and they are to submerge the hierarchical structure of the master-slave relationship beneath the fundamental *stoicheion* of the new creation: love expressing itself in mutual service (Eph 6:9 as a specific application of Gal 5:13).

The *stoicheia tou kosmou*, the forces and principles behind the ordering of this present world, are difficult to identify since the ordering of this present world is what we are socialized to take for granted from birth. It is simply difficult to question, or even know how to question, what has been presented to us from our earliest years as essentially unquestionable and self-evidently the way things need to be. The Scriptures offer a foundational resource in this task of discernment. For example, we read carefully and slowly through the sayings of Jesus; we think about what it would look like to fully embody or live out his teachings in our lives, in our faith communities, and even in the community at large. As we do so, we come across some sayings that we immediately set aside as simply impractical or that we can imagine following to a certain degree, but no further. If we are studying these texts in community, these sayings will be the ones to which we find ourselves or the person next to us objecting, "that's just not practical" or "people can't live like that in the real world." Those are the texts, then, on which we need to focus so that we may discover what is amiss in the practices, structures, logic, and priorities of "the real world"—which is also the "world" that, in its wisdom, does not know God, the "world" that is "the present, evil age"—such that they can't accommodate Jesus' teachings. The further challenge then becomes to ask what Christians need to do (and often this will entail answers in regard to what Christians-in-community need to do rather than what individual Christians on their own can do) to create alternative structures within which Jesus' teachings can be fully lived out.

For example, the encounter of Jesus with the rich young man typically evokes comments aimed at domesticating its challenge to the "realities" of practical living.

> Then someone came to him and said, "Teacher, what good deed must I do to have eternal life?" And he said to him, "Why do you ask me about what is good? There is only one who is good. If you wish to enter into life, keep the commandments." He said to him, "Which ones?" And Jesus said, "You shall not murder; You shall not commit adultery; You shall not steal; You shall not bear false witness; Honor your father and mother; also, You shall love your neighbor as yourself." The young man said to him, "I have kept all these; what do I still lack?" Jesus said to him, "If you wish to be perfect, go, sell your possessions, and give the money to the poor, and you will have treasure in heaven; then come, follow me." (Matt 19:16–21 NRSV)

First it needs to be said that it would be as radical and impractical *then* for the young man to have divested himself of his wealth to become a fellow companion of Jesus as it would be for a person to do so in the *here and now*. Often the passage is tamed by claiming that Jesus perceived that the young man had a particular problem with money, such as an unhealthy attachment to it, and so Jesus challenged him particularly on this basis. But Jesus' challenge appears rather to stem from the young man's confidence that he has in fact kept God's commandments. How can the young man claim to have truly loved his neighbor as himself when he had laid up stores of wealth for his own security against the future while neighbors of his throughout the land perished for lack of daily bread? Whence Jesus' challenge.[14]

The young man's conviction that he has kept God's commandments even while *not* actually keeping them should be taken as a cautionary tale by all would-be followers of Jesus. He was "loving his neighbor as himself" within the bounds of acting in accordance with the world's wisdom concerning the use of one's wealth, not in line with God's vision for such love, and that meant, for Jesus, that God's commandments had not yet sufficiently transformed his life to be "complete" ("perfect") in God's sight.

It is also abundantly clear from the larger Jesus tradition that this was not posed as a special challenge to a particular individual who had an unusual attachment to money. The challenge posed to the young rich man is posed to all disciples elsewhere:

> Do not store up for yourselves treasures on earth, where moth and rust consume and where thieves break in and steal; but store up for yourselves treasures in heaven, where neither moth nor rust consumes and where thieves do not break in and steal. (Matt 6:19-20 NRSV)

> Sell your possessions, and give alms. Make purses for yourselves that do not wear out, an unfailing treasure in heaven, where no thief comes near and no moth destroys. (Luke 12:33 NRSV)

The earliest Christians clearly understood the implications of these instructions. The author of 1 John asserts the incompatibility of claiming to love God (the commandment linked by Jesus with the mandate of love for neighbor) while not relieving the need of a sister or brother (1 John 3:17). The author of the *Shepherd of Hermas* seems to be commenting particularly on these words of Jesus when he writes:

---

14. The idea that giving one's wealth away to the poor to relieve their present need was a better way to provide even for one's own future need than storing it up for oneself is not novel to Jesus. It was promoted also, and centuries earlier, in Sir 29:9-12 and Tob 4:8-10. See D. A. deSilva, *The Jewish Teachers of Jesus, James, and Jude: What Earliest Christianity Learned from the Apocrypha and Pseudepigrapha* (New York and Oxford: Oxford University Press, 2012), 68-82, 93-100.

> Instead of buying lands, then, ransom souls in distress,
> as each is able. Look after widows and orphans, and don't
> neglect them. Spend your wealth and all your proper-
> ty, which you received from the Lord, upon lands and
> houses of this kind. This is why the Master made you
> rich—to fulfill these services for him. It is much better to
> buy lands, possessions, and houses of this kind, such as
> you will find in your proper city [i.e., the heavenly city],
> whenever you shall take up residence in it. (*Parable* 1.8–9,
> translation mine)

What, then, causes *us* not to respond to Jesus' commands at the level at which they encounter us? We admittedly store treasures for ourselves, perhaps in the form of saving for retirement, perhaps in the form of stockpiling nonessential goods, rather than spend this money to relieve the present needs even of *Christian* sisters and brothers now. Why? In part because the wisdom of the world has taught us from a very early age that the sensible person puts away money for later on, for retire-ment, and that it is virtually unthinkable *not* to do so if one possibly can. Employee and employer contributions to retirement accounts were part of the "package" at my seminary when I initially came on board, and indeed employee contributions were incentivized by a matching pro-gram on the employer's side. What I have currently in my TIAA–CREF account, however, could—just for one example—provide twenty-four children with support through World Vision for the next twelve years. The wisdom of the world tells me, however, that the first thing to look after is my own and my wife's ability to maintain a particular quality of life into retirement, not supporting twenty-four children on the way to self-sufficiency for their lifetime.

This is not an easy choice, even though I think it would be an obvious choice to Jesus. Faced with this choice, we are called as Christians-in-community to think about the structures or lack of structures that make it necessary to save for retirement rather than relieve current, pressing needs. A corollary *stoicheion* has to do with the essential independence of each successive generation from the preceding one—or, to put it simply, children are no longer expected to expend their resources and energies caring for their own parents after the latter can no longer support themselves. Another corollary *stoicheion* is the very idea of "retirement" rather than ongoing productivity and therefore earning potential past a particular (and rather arbitrary) age. What new structures, values, commitments, and practices could we as Christians-in-community put in place that would facilitate our responding to Jesus' vision for our use of wealth more fully?

What do we take for granted as necessary or "the way things are," just because it's what our society has inculcated us to regard as normal, necessary, or desirable?

The idea that we should all live in single-family dwellings, for instance, is hardly ever questioned, and those very few who live communally with other families under a single roof are looked upon as deviant (or communist, or whatever). But would such an arrangement enable more people to enjoy a stable dwelling rather than face foreclosure or eviction? Would such an arrangement allow families to devote a higher percentage of their collective income to the relief of people in greater need? Would such an arrangement give people greater freedom to devote themselves to various acts of ministry because there are more hands to maintain a house and there is the possibility of designating one parent out of six, rather than one out of every pair, to look after the children for an evening?

The practice of organizing "Christian" companies in hierarchical work structures with pay structures providing for vast differences in compensation for the same work or even across different kinds of work (e.g., "management" versus "labor"), just like the companies that operate in alignment with the world's wisdom, is also hardly ever questioned. Is the standard business model the proper one for such a company?

There are innumerable other points at which the *stoicheia* of our present world need to be critically examined by Christians-in-community. I don't pretend to have answers in regard to these or any other examples; the important thing is that we begin to ask these kinds of questions so that God's transformation of our lives and our communities can reach even to the structural level as we leave behind not only our "old self" or old ways of relating in the Christian community but also the old structures themselves that resist our full realignment with

God's righteousness and Christ's teaching. Living out this dimension of Paul's vision makes our lives fuller witnesses to the consummation of this transformation in the age to come.

THE TRANSFORMATION OF CREATION ITSELF

Paul looks forward not only to the transformation of individuals and of communities of people committed to Jesus, in and among whom Jesus is taking on flesh anew, but also to the transformation of the cosmos itself. In this hope he is thoroughly apocalyptic—that is to say he anticipates a cosmic transformation no less than does the prophet John who gave us the Revelation (see especially 21:1–22:5) or 2 Peter with its vision of cosmic conflagration and renewal (2 Pet 3:7–13).

Paul articulates this hope most fully in a digression in Romans 8, talking about the challenges of living in the tension between the initiation of God's remarkable transformation of people, community, and cosmos and the fulfillment of the same:

> The creation waits with eager longing for the revealing of the children of God; for the creation was subjected to futility, not of its own will but by the will of the one who subjected it, in hope that the creation itself will be set free from its bondage to decay and will obtain the freedom of the glory of the children of God. We know that the whole creation has been groaning in labor pains until now; and not only the creation, but we ourselves, who have the first fruits of the Spirit, groan inwardly while we wait for adoption, the redemption of our bodies. For in hope we were saved. (Rom 8:19–24a NRSV)

Paul speaks of a mystical interconnection between the transformation of the individual into the likeness of Christ's glory and the transformation of the cosmos itself. Our mortal bodies are themselves part of "creation," so the interconnection is endemic to our nature as created beings, an integral part of the larger creation of God. Our groaning for God's consummation is a groaning shared sympathetically throughout the physical creation; the final destruction of "death" (see 1 Cor 15:25–26) means the good news of renewal and liberation not only for "our bodies" but also the whole creation.

According to Paul, the fall did not merely affect human beings but creation (or "Nature") itself. Not only are individuals and human societies and structures out of alignment with God's good purposes, but nature itself has been compromised. Like human beings, creation itself is sentenced to "futility," to come to nothing, to fail to attain God's good for it—ultimately to be subjected to the same death-dealing and death-bound forces as mortal humanity. "Death" is at work throughout creation even as it is in our mortal bodies. All animal life dies and rots. Over the course of Paul's travels, he saw long stretches of nonarable land that recalled the primeval curse (as in Gen 3:17) and the lengths to which people had to go to make land arable. Earthquakes and seaquakes (with their resultant flood swells) were common enough phenomena in the eastern Mediterranean, and perhaps Paul had such upheavals in mind as he reflected on the groaning, the heaving sighs, of creation itself as it awaited renewal and transformation. The Mediterranean Sea, impassible from October through March, was itself a constant witness to creation's upheaval and disorder. Just twenty-some years after Paul wrote Romans, Vesuvius would bury two thriving cities in a dramatic testimony to creation's subjection to disorder and death. Part of Paul's "good news"—a muted part, to be sure, but a part nonetheless—is this hope that creation or "nature" itself would be freed from its bondage to decay and the death-dealing forces at work in this present, evil age.

The question of theodicy—where is God's justice when tragedy strikes—is one of the most complex and one of the most important facing human beings. Whether a person continues in his or her faith often depends on finding adequate answers to this question in the midst of difficult times. I will not presume to address the larger question, but I will suggest that Paul's conception of creation itself being subjected to futility, to decay, to the power of death alongside our mortal bodies, and the conception of creation itself groaning with us in the midst of our mutual subjection to death-bound forces, might contribute to addressing the larger question.

The 2004 tsunami that claimed 200,000 lives and displaced another 1.5 million across southeast Asia was not an act of violence that God perpetrated upon human beings. It was not something that even Nature did willingly. It was a sign of the subjection of Nature itself to death and futility, an event at which Nature herself groaned, longing for God's redemption of humanity and creation itself. The baby who is born with a congenital defect that claims her life before it has begun, or who is born with a debilitating condition that will challenge his existence over the course of a long life, is not the victim of God's capriciousness, but a causality of Nature subjected itself to such futility and decay, over whom Nature groans alongside the parents, longing for God's redemption of our condition. In both, God's own Spirit notably also groans "with sighs inexpressible" (Rom 8:26), not willing the tragedy, but joining with those who pray and long for the day of consummation.

The "good news" is that redemption, inclusive of the entire kosmos currently gone awry, will indeed happen. When the new humanity formed in Christ is transformed from mortality to immortality, creation itself will participate in the glorious liberation of the children of God from all the forces of death—when, in the words of John Donne, "Death, thou shalt die."[15] For now the new humanity in Christ must hope—and this not passively as people waiting, but actively as people longing, who are themselves investing fully in embracing the transformation God is working out as the way forward to the resolution of all present ills.

> Now, in the meanwhile, with hearts raised on high,
> We for that country must yearn and must sigh;
> Seeking Jerusalem, dear native land,
> Through our long exile on Babylon's strand.[16]

---

15. John Donne, "Death Be Not Proud," published in *Songs and Sonnets*, 1633; see also 1 Cor 15:26.
16. From Peter Abelard's poem *"O quanta qualia sunt illa Sabbata,"* trans. John M. Neale. in *Hymnal Noted*, ed. J. M. Neale and Thomas Helmore (London, 1854; repr., Glendale, CO: Lancelot Andrewes Press, 2010). The hymn "O What Their Joy and Their Glory Must Be" appears in many modern hymnals in use in mainline denominations.

INDEXES

Subject and Author Index

A

Abelard, Peter 113 n. 16
Abraham 51–3, 53 n. 8, 58–9
Adam 33
adoption 68–9, 111
alcohol 86
Antioch Conflict 81
apocalypticism 95, 111
Apollos 84
Aristotle 76, 82, 87
assurance of salvation 34, 35–38, 55, 55 n. 9, 58 n. 11
atonement 46; see also penal substitution
authority (secular) 102–4
    in marriage, see hierarchy of genders
authorship:
    of 1 and 2 Timothy 35 n. 39
    of Colossians 35 n. 39, 88 n. 12
    of Ephesians 14 n. 8, 88 n. 12
    of Titus 35 n. 39

B

Bailey, Daniel 46
Balch, David 88 n. 11
baptism 17 n. 9, 18, 21, 70

infant versus credo-baptism 85–86
Barclay, J. M. G. 60 n. 15, 62 n. 19, 81 n. 7
Bauer, Walter 25 n. 19, 25 n. 21, 27 n. 27, 75 n. 5, 95 n. 2
Beilby, James 24 n. 18, 46 n. 1
Beker, J. Christiaan 95 n. 4
belief 10, 20, 23, 44, 50, 52, 58 n. 11, 59, 64; see also faith
benefaction, see patronage
Betz, Hans D. 60 n. 14, 62 n. 19
Bird, Michael 9 n. 3, 20 n. 13, 22 n. 15, 23 n. 16, 24 n. 18, 27 n. 28, 30 n. 32, 58 n. 11, 60 n. 15
body of Christ 68–72; see also family
Boers, Hendrickus 17 n. 9
Bruce, F. F. 11 n. 5, 12 n. 6
Burrhus 103

C

Calvin, John 85
Cephas, see Peter
Christ, see Jesus
Christology 23 n. 16

Church 18, 68, 72, 73, 76, 77, 80, 81, 84, 91; *see also* body of Christ; family (of God)
   early church 76
   salvation outside of 91–2
Cicero 17 n. 10
circumcision 14, 17, 18, 29, 30, 31, 50, 52, 56, 82, 104, 105; *see also* uncircumcision
Clement 75
clothing 13, 53–4, 56
communal property 76–7, 110
community 67–92, 106, 110
   of faith 3, 5, 6, 17, 22, 73, 74, 82, 106; *see also* family (of God)
confession of faith 1, 3, 10, 18, 21, 23, 30, 38, 76, 85
conversion of household 87
Corinth 13, 84
Cornelius 87
cosmos 5, 6, 16, 17, 93–7, 98, 111, 113; *see also* stoicheia tou kosmou
covenant 17, 65; *see also* new covenant *and* community of faith
cross 5, 35, 46, 47, 49, 55 n. 9, 81, 96
crucifixion 34, 47, 55 n. 9, 66, 96; *see also* death of Jesus
   co-crucifixion with Jesus 10–11, 39, 47, 55–56, 59, 61, 104
   crucifixion of the flesh 45, 59

D

Danker, Frederick 25 n. 19, 25 n. 21, 27 n. 27, 75 n. 5, 95 n. 2
day of Christ 14, 32; *see also* final judgment
death 1, 2, 3, 20, 27 n. 28, 64, 85, 96 n. 5, 111, 112–13

   of Jesus 4, 5, 11, 12, 13, 14, 15, 19 n. 12, 21, 29, 36, 39, 45, 46–7, 59, 79
   to the old self 54, 56, 57–8, 59
   to the Torah/law 10
   fear of 63–6
deliverance 16, 20, 23, 31, 35–38, 42, 45, 46, 51, 55 n. 9, 56, 58, 75, 104, 111, 113; *see also* forgiveness
   from the power of sin 60–1
denominationalism 84
deSilva, David 6 n. 4, 11 n. 5, 12 n. 6, 14 n. 8, 35 n. 39, 40 n. 44, 50 n. 5, 57 n. 10, 69 n. 2, 81 n. 7, 88 n. 11, 99 n. 7, 103 n. 11, 108 n. 14
Diaspora 81 n. 7
discipleship 5, 22, 41–42, 63, 84
disobedience 18, 21, 33, 36, 55
diversity 85–6
Donne, John 38, 113
Dunn, James D. G. 11 n. 5, 12 n. 6, 61 n. 17

E

Eddy, Paul 24 n. 18, 46 n. 1
ekklēsia, see Church
election 17
Engberg-Pedersen, Troels 60 n. 15
Ephesus 35
eternal life 2, 3, 4, 12, 13, 16, 22, 38, 49, 63, 65, 107; *see also* glorification
ethnic divisions 80–4; *see also* social divisions; gender divisions
ethnic identity 80–1
Euodia 75

F

faith 5, 8, 9 n. 3, 10, 11, 13, 15, 20, 23 n. 16, 29, 30, 31, 34, 35, 38, 40, 43,

46, 50, 51, 52, 53, 55 n. 9, 68, 72,
73, 74, 77, 79, 85, 87, 91, 93, 106,
112; *see also* belief
the fall 112
family 73, 87–91, 110
of God 25 n. 21, 68–9, 76–7, 83
favoritism
of God 14–19, 24, 90
in Greco-Roman culture 17–18
Feldman, Louis H. 81 n. 7
Ferguson, Everett 82 n. 9
the flesh 20, 22, 22 n. 15, 30, 40, 59,
60, 62, 74, 85
forgiveness 1, 2, 8, 13, 32, 44, 45, 47,
48, 104; *see also* reconciliation
in the family of God 69, 74–6
freedom 31, 42, 44–53, 89, 111, 113
from the power of sin 60–2, 67
Fronto (Roman senator) 17, 17 n. 10

G
Gabba, Emilio 81 n. 7
Galatia 28, 58, 81
Garland, David 70 n. 3
Garlington, Don 60 n. 16
Gathercole, Simon 8 n. 2, 27 n. 28
gender divisions 80–4; *see
also* social divisions;
ethnic divisions
gender inclusive language 69 n. 1
Gentile(s) 12, 16, 29, 30, 31, 50, 61,
67, 76, 80–1, 84, 97, 100; *see also*
Jew; Greek
glorification 8, 13, 38, 66, 97, 111
Gorman, Michael 24 n. 18
grace 2, 4, 8, 16, 17, 19 n. 12, 29, 33,
36, 38–43, 38 n. 41, 44, 45, 46, 47,
50, 51, 75, 80, 84
gratitude 41, 43, 45, 56, 62, 89
Greco-Roman social customs 39–41,
81 n. 7, 82, 88 n. 11, 91

Greek (people) 15, 16, 18, 56, 70, 78;
see also Gentile; Jew

H
hierarchy:
of genders 88; *see also*
submission of wives
to husbands
social 97–8, 110
hilastērion, see mercy seat
holiness 7, 9 n. 3, 14, 48–50, 58
n. 11, 65
Holy Spirit 5, 9 n. 3, 15, 20, 22, 22
n. 15, 23, 23 n. 16, 27 n. 27, 27
n. 28, 28, 29, 30 n. 32, 31, 32, 33,
34, 35, 42, 43, 48, 50, 54, 68, 75,
85, 86, 105, 111, 113
gifts of, *see* spiritual gifts
giving of 2, 5, 15, 20, 28, 42, 48,
49, 58–63, 67
guidance of 43, 53–4, 56, 57,
58, 73
honor 16, 42, 69, 83, 85, 86, 97, 107
hope 26, 44, 46, 49, 51, 65, 77, 111,
112, 113
hospitality 87
household of faith, *see* community
of faith
household of God, *see* community
of faith
humility 56, 79–80, 98

I
idol(s) 16, 78, 100
incarnation 50
individualism 67–8, 93
in Christ 12, 13, 14, 28, 29, 30 n. 32,
34, 68, 85
image of God 14, 50
Jesus as 50
Israel, people of 17, 18, 30

idolatry 20, 21, 55, 97

J

Jesus:
    first coming 20, 30
    second coming 36, 103–4
Jew(s) 15, 16, 17, 19, 29, 30, 46, 50,
    52, 56, 59 n. 12, 61, 67, 70, 76, 78,
    80–1, 84, 86, 97, 100; see also
    Gentile; Greek
Jewish, see Jew(s)
John Calvin, see Calvin, John
Johnson, Luke Timothy 35 n. 39
Josephus 25 n. 19, 26 n. 25
Judea 15
Judaism 23 n. 16, 66, 81 n. 7
judgment 16, 20, 85–6, 102
    of God 15–19, 26
    by works 22, 28 n. 29
    final 1, 6, 10, 12, 15, 16, 17, 19, 24,
        27, 29 n. 31, 33, 34, 44, 55
        n. 9, 85
judgment seat 15
justice of God 17, 18, 19
justification 2, 7–9, 10, 11, 15, 19 n. 12,
    2, 23 n. 16, 24–34, 37, 38 n. 41, 44,
    46, 47, 52, 55 n. 9, 58 n. 11, 59, 67

K

kingdom of God 18, 20, 21, 50, 80,
    94, 95, 104–6
Kinnaman, David 18 n. 11
Kraybill, Nelson 103 n. 11

L

last day, see final judgment
law 5, 22 n. 15, 28 n. 29, 29, 31, 60
    n. 15, 62, 68, 81, 103
    of Christ, see law of God
    of God 29 n. 31, 30, 31, 61, 62, 73
    of sin 62

liturgy 86–7
Long, A. A. 70 n. 3
Longenecker, Richard 11 n. 5, 12 n. 6,
    60 n. 14
love 8, 9 n. 3, 14, 29, 30, 31, 32, 33,
    39, 40, 56, 71, 79, 89, 91, 103, 106,
    107, 108
    of Christ 39, 30
    of God 3, 11, 33, 43, 45, 46, 58
        n. 11, 67
Luther, Martin 9, 37, 85
Lydia 87
Lyons, Gabe 18 n. 11

M

manna 76
Marcus Aurelius 17
Martin Luther, see Luther, Martin
Martyn, J. Louis 99 n. 8
mercy seat 46–7
militarism 101
millennial generation 18
Moses:
    Mosaic covenant 13
    Mosaic Law, see Torah
Moxnes, Halvor 88 n. 11

N

Nero 103
new birth 35, 38; see also
    new creation
new covenant 13
new creation 2, 8, 9, 14, 26 n. 25, 31
    n. 34, 46, 48, 49, 50, 54, 64, 92,
    104–5, 106, 112
new life 2, 11, 27 n. 27, 43,
    50–1, 53, 54, 92, 102; see also
    new creation

O

obedience 9 n. 3, 12, 16, 17, 31, 33, 52,
55 n. 9, 66, 76
of Jesus 12, 33, 37, 58 n. 11
to the Torah/law 25
of slaves to masters 90
Onesimus 82-3
Onesiphorus 87
order of salvation 9, 9 n. 4,
ordo salutis, see order of salvation
Origen 91-2
Osiek, Carolyn 88 n. 11

P

parousia, see Jesus, second coming
partiality of God, *see* favoritism
of God
partisanship 84-7
patronage 39-40, 97
penal substitution 46, 46 n. 1
Peter 81, 84, 103, 111
Philemon 82-3
Philippi 37, 79
prayer 57
profession of faith, *see* confession
of faith
promise(s) of God 4-5, 46, 51-2,
58, 59
Protestant(s) 2, 6, 9, 30 n. 33, 50, 68

R

Räisänen, H. 22 n. 15
Ramachandra, Vinoth 101 n. 9
reciprocity (Greco-Roman
social custom) 39-41; *see
also* patronage
reconciliation:
in the family of God 69,
73, 74-6
to God 1, 2, 10, 33, 36-7, 46, 67,
redemption, *see* deliverance

Reformation 6, 7, 8, 28, 38, 58 n. 11
regeneration, *see* new birth
Reinhold, Meyer 81 n. 7
repentance 16
resurrection:
general 20, 66, 77
of Jesus 5, 11, 13, 14, 20, 26
n. 27, 37
retirement 76, 109-10
revolution 102, 103-6
righteousness 2, 15, 24, 25-9, 30-33,
44, 52, 59, 61
of God 10, 11, 13, 15, 17, 22, 26
n. 25, 27, 30, 31, 32, 44, 58
n. 11, 61, 110-11
of Jesus 19, 27
by means of works 8, 28,
29-30, 48
rights 78-9
Romans Road 3-4, 9
Rome 1, 51 n. 7, 82, 103
Ryle, J. C. 8

S

Sabbath 86
sacraments 84, 87
sanctification 7-9, 21, 28
Sanders, E. P. 22 n. 15
Sarah (wife of Abraham) 52
Schlatter, Adolf 9 n. 4
Schrenk, Gottlob 23 n. 16, 25 n. 19,
25 n. 22, 26 n. 23, 26 n. 25, 27
n. 26, 28 n. 30
Seifrid, Mark 9, 9 n. 4, 24 n. 18, 26
n. 25, 27 n. 26, 34 n. 37, 48 n. 3,
53 n. 8
Seneca 40, 41, 103
sexual immorality 20, 21, 36, 55
sin 1, 3, 5, 10, 19 n. 12, 22, 26, 28
n. 30, 32, 33, 42, 46, 47, 49, 61, 67,
74, 96 n. 5, 104

origin of 33–4
power of 60–2
slavery 82–3, 90, 98, 100
    illegitimacy of 90–1
Snodgrass, Klyne 8, 8 n. 2, 31 n. 34
social change 93–4, 100–1, 102–11
social divisions 80–4, 99, 105, 106
Spicq, Ceslaus 25 n. 19, 25 n. 20, 32 n. 35
Spirit, *see* Holy Spirit
spiritual disciplines 56–7
spiritual gifts 71–2
Stephanas of Corinth 87
Stewart, David J. 4 n. 3
stoicheia tou kosmou 98–102, 105, 106, 109, 110
Stoicism 70, 72
submission:
    of wife to husband 89–90; *see also* hierarchy of genders
    mutual 88–90
Syntyche 75

T
Talbert, Charles 28 n. 29, 28 n. 30, 47 n. 2, 61 n. 18
Teamoh, George 82
thankfulness, *see* gratitude
theodicy 112–3
Torah 10–1, 12, 14, 18, 25 n. 19, 28, 29, 31, 39, 52, 60, 60 n. 15, 61, 62, 84, 86, 98, 100
    curse of 58
trust, *see* belief

U
uncircumcision 18, 29, 31, 45, 50, 52, 56, 82, 104, 105
unity 84–7

V
Vesuvius 112

W
Watts, Isaac 43
Wesley, John 9 n. 3, 57, 84
White, Dale C. 101 n. 9
Wilson, Bryan 102, 102 n. 10
Wink, Walter 101 n. 9
wisdom 96–8, 107, 119, 110
Witherington, Ben, III 11 n. 5
the world 18, 19, 23, 68, 69, 83, 85, 94–100 , 106–7; *see also* cosmos
worship, styles of 86–7
wrath of God 15, 16, 21, 31, 38, 46, 55, 103
Wright, N. T. 22 n. 15, 23 n. 16, 23 n. 17, 24 n. 18, 25 n. 21, 27 n. 28, 29 n. 31, 30 n. 33, 33–4, 34 n. 37, 34 n. 38, 38 n. 41, 39 n. 43, 58 n. 11, 59 n. 12, 93 n. 1

Scripture Index

Old Testament

Genesis
3:17......................112
15:6.........................52

Exodus...................46
16:14-21................76
16:18.......................76

Leviticus................46
11:44...............82 n. 8
11:45...............82 n. 8

19:2.................82 n. 8
20:7.................82 n. 8
20:22-26.........82 n. 8
20:24...............82 n. 8

Deuteronomy
27:26.....................59

2 Chronicles
19:7.........................19

Psalms
32:1-2....................47

Isaiah
52:5.........................18

Habakkuk
2:4...........................15

New Testament

Matthew
5:45.........................25
6:19-20................108
7:21-23.................18
9:13.........................25
9:16-21................107
13:41.....................25
13:49.....................25
23:28.....................25

Mark
2:17.........................25
8:34-5....................58
8:35.........................66
10:42-44...............97

Luke
1:17.........................25
5:32.........................25
12:33.....................108

15:7.........................25
20:20.....................25

Acts
10:24......................87
10:34......................19
10:47-8.................87
16:15......................87
16:27-34...............87
18:12-16......103 n. 11

24:15......................25

Romans........ 4, 15, 17
   n. 9, 36, 87, 103
   n. 11, 112
1:6....................31, 53
1:16-18..................15
1:18-21..................45
1:18-32..................97
1:24-25..................45
1:28......................45
2-3.......................24
2:1-11..........28 n. 29
2:1-16..........20 n. 13
2:2-11..................17
2:6-11..................19
2:7................28 n. 29
2:10..............28 n. 29
2:11..................14, 19
2:12................28 n. 29
2:13................28 n. 29
2:23-4..................18
2:25......................18
3:9......................61
3:20..............28 n. 29
3:23....................3, 46
3:24......................44
3:26..................24, 58
3:27-28........30 n. 33
3:27-30..................30
3:27-31..................52
3:28.............. 23 n. 16,
   30 n. 33
3:29-30.........30 n. 33
4..........................51
4:1-12..................47
4:4......................24
4:4-5....................30

4:5..........................48
4:5-8.....................19
4:9.........................52
4:11-13.................30
4:18-22.................52
4:20.................53 n. 8
5:1...........................3
5:6-7......................25
5:9...........................3
5:9-10...............36-7
5:12.......................33
5:17.........................2
5:19..................25, 33
5:21.......................25
6:1-23...................12
6:4........................56
6:6........................61
6:13........................4
6:14......................61
6:16-20.........25 n. 21
6:17-18.................61
6:23......................2, 3
7:4...................69 n. 1
7:7........................61
7:7-25.............. 60-2,
   61 n. 18
7:14......................61
7:18-19.................61
7:24......................62
7:25......................62
8............ 22 n. 15, 111
8:1......... 3, 5, 22 n. 15
8:2........................62
8:4............. 5, 60 n. 15
8:5-8.............58 n. 11
8:5-9......................63
8:11......................20
8:13..............22 n. 15

8:13-14..................20
8:14......................20
8:19-24.................111
8:26.....................113
8:28......................14
8:29......................14
8:38-9...........58 n. 11
10:2-4...................15
10:3......................31
10:9..................3, 23
11:35.....................40
12:1-2..... 13, 58 n. 11
12:2..................104-5
12:5......................69
12:5-8...................71
12:10....................83
12:16....................83
13:1-7................ 104
13:1-8..............102-3
13:8-10 ....31, 60
   n. 15, 62
13:11.................. 104
13:11-14.................36
14:2-6...................86
14:10.............20 n. 13
14:13-15............78-9
14:19-21............78-9
15:18......................31
16:1-2....................87
16:3-5....................87
16:23......................87
16:25-6...................21
16:26......................53

1 Corinthians..13 n. 7
1:8-9......................32
1:12......................84
1:16......................87

1:18....................35, 97
1:18–25...................96
1:20.................96 n. 5
1:21..........................96
1:22–24..................97
3:3–4......................84
3:18–19..............95–6
4:3–5.............28 n. 29
5:9...................13 n. 7
6:9–11.....................21
6:11................23 n. 16
6:15.........................53
6:20.........................42
7:19................17, 31
7:29–31.................105
9:24–7.....................54
10:23–34.................78
11:20–22.................83
12:7–12...................71
12:12–14..................70
12:27......................70
12:32–33.................78
13:12......................85
14:26...............69 n. 1
14:36...............69 n. 1
15:24.................. 104
15:25–6.................121
15:29–30................65
15:32......................65
15:54......................63
15:58........ 63, 69 n. 1
16:19......................87

2 Corinthians.........13
2:1–4.............. 13 n. 7
2:9...................13 n. 7
2:14–6:13......39 n. 43
2:10–15.........20 n. 13

3:9................26 n. 24
3:18......................13
4:16–18..................66
5:10............. 20 n. 13,
    28 n. 29
5:14–15.........39 n. 43
5:14–21.........39 n. 43
5:15.....4, 39, 39 n. 43,
    42, 43, 97
5:17.................14, 50
6:1.............................2
7:8................. 13 n. 7
8:13–15..................76
9:13........................76
11:2........................68
11:9................ 69 n. 1
11:25......... 103 n. 11

Galatians 12, 17
    n. 9, 28, 29, 59
    n. 12
1:4...................95 n. 3
1:5...................95 n. 3
1:19–20..................97
2:11–14...................81
2:15–16.........59 n. 12
2:15–18....................11
2:16...............28 n. 29
2:19.................53, 72
2:19–20......................
    10–11, 12, 23 n. 16,
    39 n. 43, 42, 49
2:21..... 2, 26 n. 24, 59
3:1–5.......................34
3:2.................23 n. 16
3:2–5.............59 n. 12
3:3..........................15
3:5.................23 n. 16

3:6–9.......................52
3:10–14..................97
3:13–14..............58–9
3:14...........2, 23 n. 16,
    59 n. 12
3:21..........................59
3:28................82, 105
4:1–5...................98–9
4:1–11....................98
4:6–7.............59 n. 12
4:8–11..................98–9
4:11.......................100
4:12................ 69 n. 1
4:19... 12, 23 n. 16, 39
    n. 43, 49
4:28................ 69 n. 1
4:31................ 69 n. 1
5:2–4.......................52
5:5..........................59
5:5–6............ 23 n. 16,
    29, 29 n. 31
5:6...........17, 31 n. 34
5:11................. 69 n. 1
5:13..........89, 91, 106
5:13–14........ 29 n. 31,
    31, 62
5:16......... 60, 60 n. 13
5:16–17..................59
5:17.........................60
5:16–25...................15
5:19–21.............21, 22
5:24–25...................59
5:25................60 n. 15
6:1............................74
6:2................ 29 n. 31
6:7–10.....................22
6:15............ 14, 17, 50
6:17.......................66

Ephesians ...... 14 n. 8,
   35 n. 39
1:4 32
1:21 .... 95 n. 3
2:1–2 .... 95 n. 3,
   96 n. 5
2:3 49
2:7 .... 95 n. 3
2:8 35
2:10 50–1
2:11–16 81
2:22 81
3:12 47
4:11–13 71
4:15–16 71
4:17–18 54
4:22–24 ...... 13–14, 54
4:30–1 75
5:5–6 21
5:18–23 89
5:21 .... 89, 90, 91
5:21–6:4 88
5:22 .... 89, 90
6:5–9 90
6:7 91
6:8 90
6:9 .... 19, 106
6:12 101

Philippians
1:6 .... 14, 32
1:9–11 32
1:11 32
1:12 .... 69 n. 1
2:1–11 98
2:2–4 89
2:3–4 79

2:5–11 12
2:12–13 37
2:13 33
3:8–11 11
3:9 .... 15, 31, 44
3:10–15 37
3:13 .... 69 n. 1
3:20–1 63
4:2–3 75
4:8 .... 69 n. 1
4:21 .... 69 n. 1

Colossians .....35 n. 39
1:13–14 104
1:14 45
1:15 50
1:21–3 32
2:8 .... 98, 99
2:13–14 .... 45, 47
2:20–22 .... 98, 99
3:5–17 55–6
3:11 82
3:13 75
3:18–4:1 87
3:25 19
4:10 87

1 Thessalonians 77
3:13 32
4:10 .... 69 n. 1
4:18 77
5:3 104
5:4 .... 69 n. 1
5:11 77
5:14 .... 69 n. 1
5:23 32

2 Thessalonians
3:16 .... 69 n. 1

1 Timothy .....35 n. 39
1:9 25

2 Timothy .....35 n. 39
1:16 87
4:19 87

Titus .... 35 n. 39
2:11–14 51
3:3–8 48–9
3:4–5 35

Philemon
2 87
15–16 .... 83, 106
22 87

2 Peter
3:7–13 111

1 John
3:17 108

Revelation.... 103, 111
21:1–22:5 111

Apocrypha and Pseudepigrapha

1 Enoch
63:8........................19

Sirach
29:9–12.......108 n. 14
35:14–16................19

Testament of Job
4:7...........................19
43:13.......................19

Tobit
4:8–10..................108

Wisdom of Solomon
1:16.........................65
2:1–2......................64
2:6–11....................64
2:22–3....................65
13:1–2..................100

13:1–9.....................97
14:22–31................97

Other Ancient Texts

Aristotle
Nichomachean Ethics
8.9.1 ....76 n. 6
Politics
1.12 87–8
1.4 ....82 n. 9

Cicero
Ad Familiares
13 ....18 n. 10

Dio Chrysostom
Rhodaica
37 41

Fronto
Ad Marcum Caesarem
3.2 ....18 n. 10

Josephus
Against Apion
2.293 ....25 n. 19
Jewish Antiquities
6.165 ....25 n. 19
8.208 ....25 n. 19

Origen
Homilies on Joshua
3:5 91

Philo
De via contemplativa
3 100
De Decalogo
53 100

Seneca
On Benefits
1.3.2–5 41
1.4.2 40
2.25.3...................41
3.1.1 41

Shepherd of Hermas
Parable 1.8–9 ...108–9

Sophocles
Ajax 522.................41